Praise for Drew Curtis and *It's Not News, It's Fark*:

"Fark is for: fans of *The Daily Show, News of the Weird*. Fark is not for: the squeamish." —*The Washington Post*

"Drew Curtis knows his crap." —*Playboy*

"A funny book.... also a sharp and well-deserved criticism of the news media—and life in a capitalistic, all-information, all-the-time world." —CNN.com

"Explains the workings of mass media better than most insider accounts. Funnier (and quicker) than a two-year stint in journalism school." —Wired.com

"*It's Not News, It's Fark* does more to advance the journalistic art than all the millions spent by the Poynter Institute, the Shorenstein Center, the Nieman Foundation, the Project for Excellence in Journalism, the *Columbia Journalism Review* and the *American Journalism Review*, the Committee of Concerned Journalists, the various Annenberg outposts, and the Freedom Forum, combined." —Slate.com

"Curtis delivers [his critique] with richly sarcastic humor." —*Publishers Weekly*

"You don't have to have a journalism degree from Columbia to pull aside the curtain and show everyone that there's no wizard—you just have to be a reasonably intelligent guy who lives and breathes news." —*New York Press*

"The right book at the right time.... I laughed, I cried, I wised up. In fact, at one point I laughed so hard I almost threw up. Readers who want to know where that happened need to buy this book and read the item about Homeland Security and goats."

—Stephen King

"As a member of the news media, I can state authoritatively that this book will cure cancer AND end global warming."

—Dave Barry, humorist and bestselling author

"*It's Not News, It's Fark* is an insightful examination of how mass media is drowning in filler and fluff. Still, it could have used a chapter on Boobies."

—*The Smoking Gun*

BROOKS MELCHIOR

Drew Curtis founded Fark.com after several beers one night in 1999. Today it averages 3.5 to 5 million people per month depending on whether or not he posts links about Britney Spears not wearing underwear. Media corporations worldwide continue to use Fark as a resource to judge which stories are newsworthy. He has been featured in *Time, The Washington Post, PC Magazine, Maxim, FHM,* and *Playboy,* on hundreds of radio stations around the country, and was recently on the cover of *Business 2.0.* He lives in Lexington, Kentucky, with his wife and two children.

It's Not News, It's
FARK

How Mass Media Tries to Pass Off Crap as News

DREW CURTIS

GOTHAM BOOKS

GOTHAM BOOKS
Published by Penguin Group (USA) Inc.
375 Hudson Street, New York, New York 10014, U.S.A.

Penguin Group (Canada),90 Eglinton Avenue East, Suite 700, Toronto, Ontario, Canada M4P
2Y3 (a division of Pearson Penguin Canada Inc.); Penguin Books Ltd, 80 Strand, London
WC2R ORL, England; Penguin Ireland, 25 St Stephen's Green, Dublin 2, Ireland (a division of
Penguin Books Ltd); Penguin Group (Australia), 250 Camberwell Road, Camberwell, Victoria
3124, Australia (a division of Pearson Australia Group Pty Ltd); Penguin Books India Pvt Ltd,
11 Community Centre, Panchsheel Park, New Delhi–110 017, India; Penguin Group (NZ),
67 Apollo Drive, Rosedale, North Shore 0632, New Zealand (a division of Pearson New Zealand
Ltd); Penguin Books (South Africa) (Pty) Ltd, 24 Sturdee Avenue, Rosebank, Johannesburg
2196, South Africa

Penguin Books Ltd, Registered Offices: 80 Strand, London WC2R ORL, England

Published by Gotham Books, a member of Penguin Group (USA) Inc.

Previously published as a Gotham Books hardcover edition

First trade paperback printing, June 2008

10 9 8 7 6 5 4 3 2 1

Gotham Books and the skyscraper logo are trademarks of Penguin Group (USA) Inc.

The Library of Congress has cataloged the hardcover edition of this book as follows:
Curtis, Drew.
    It's not news, it's fark : how mass media tries to pass off crap as news / Drew Curtis.
        p. cm.
    ISBN 978-1-592-40291-5 (hardcover)   ISBN 978-1-592-40366-0 (paperback)
    1. Mass media—United States.   I. Title.
P92.U5C87 2007
302.23—dc22   2007008151

Printed in the United States of America
Set in Janson MT with Abadi MT
Designed by Sabrina Bowers

To Heather, without whom I wouldn't be able to keep my detail stuff straight. Thanks for running interference so I had the time to finish the book. All my love.

To Storm, who was very patient through this process, sitting in my chair and waiting until I was done so we could play with trains.

To Chance, who moved in suddenly during the tail end of the process and basically just sat around eating, sleeping, and pooping. Here's hoping that behavior doesn't repeat when you graduate college in 22+ years.

Contents

It's Not News, It's
FARK

What Is Fark?

FARK IS WHAT FILLS SPACE WHEN MASS MEDIA RUNS OUT OF news. It's not news, it's Fark. Fark is supposed to look like news...but it's not news.

There is an ancient (supposed) Chinese curse: "May you live in interesting times." Let's face it, interesting times suck. Whenever Mass Media is really fulfilling its intended purpose, generally something bad is going on. Wars, blown elections, bad weather, you name it—when people need to know something, it's probably because it's likely to kill them. We'd be much better off living in non-interesting times.

Not living in interesting times presents a problem for Mass Media, however. This has been further compounded by the advent of twenty-four-hour news channels and the Internet as a news source. Back in the days when TV news concentrated most of its resources on a half-hour block of news, finding material to fill the time slot wasn't difficult. Nowadays cable news networks have to scramble to have something to talk about twenty-four hours a day, even when nothing of import is going on. Sales departments are still selling advertisements, after all. Mass Media can't just run content made entirely of ads (with the possible exception of the Home Shopping Network). Something has to fill the space.

Over the years Mass Media has developed several methods of filling this space. No one teaches this in journalism school; odds are Mass Media itself hasn't given much thought to the process. It's a practice honed over the years by editors and publishers, verbally passed down from one generation to the next. They're not entirely aware they're doing it, although the media folks who read advance copies of this manuscript all had the same reaction: "I've been saying we should stop doing this for YEARS."

ENTER FARK

Let's get this one out of the way: Fark.com isn't a Weblog. Mass Media has categorized Fark.com as a blog, but it's not. The word *Weblog* seems to have been defined by Mass Media as anything news-related that is not Mass Media. If you asked them, they'd tell you a Weblog was everything from sites actually producing news commentary to guys in their pajamas talking about what they ate for dinner. Some so-called Weblogs have offices and employees. When did we stop calling these magazines? The only difference is the lack of a hard-copy print version of the Web site.

Fark.com, the Web site, is a news aggregator, an edited community-driven news site. Every day Fark receives 2,000 or so news submissions from its readership. I pore over them and decide what to put up on the Web site; usually this is based on how funny the submitted tagline is more than anything else. The tagline is essentially the article headline rewritten into a one-line joke by the submitter, attracting readers to the article link. For example: original headline—"Brain Power." It's an article about how species with larger brains need to consume more food to power their brains. Fark tagline—"Study shows the bigger your brain, the more energy you consume. This explains how Paris Hilton can survive on a diet of alcohol and semen." As you can see, the end result is much improved, and sometimes more accurate.

Fark isn't an acronym. It doesn't mean anything. The idea was to have the word *Fark* come to symbolize news that is really Not News. Hence the slogan "It's not news, it's Fark." It never caught on. So it goes.

Fark was originally a word I became known for using online back in the early 1990s. Damned if I can remember why. I think it was either to replace another F-word or I was just drunk and mistyped something. I tell everyone it was the former; it's a better story that way.

I lived in Great Britain my junior year of college, in Nottingham to be exact. When I returned from the United Kingdom in 1994, few people had an e-mail address. My friend Phil had one until he left university, after which we switched to snail mail to keep contact. Being average guys, we were horrible at keeping in touch via snail mail. For a while we were trading letters probably once every six months, and that's being generous. I spent the mid-1990s starting an Internet service provider (ISP) from scratch; Phil spent at least part of the nineties volunteering for medical experiments for cash. He really did. I'm not sure which of us came out ahead on his respective venture.

Fark.com initially sprang to life from the back-and-forth correspondence Phil and I sporadically sent each other. I have no idea when it started, but I began dropping in the occasional weird news story from America. One of the first ones I remember, if not the actual first one, was a news story about a fighter plane crash over New Mexico or Nevada. The crash was caused when one of the pilots, flying within feet of another jet as air force pilots do when on maneuvers or invading other countries' airspace, took off his flight suit to moon the other pilot. They were high enough up that he lost consciousness due to lack of oxygen and crashed.

In the summer of 1997, I remember having a conversation with another friend, Mike, who ran the servers and other equipment for the ISP and still runs the servers for Fark. He made a comment about how all the four-letter domain names were disappearing quickly. On a whim I checked to see if Fark.com was available. It was; I grabbed it.

At the time the only thing you could do with a Web site was put up what was then called a vanity site. This was what almost all the Internet consisted of back in 1997. Think of vanity sites as poorly coded MySpace pages. Yes, MySpace pages look pretty bad, but these were worse. I didn't want to use the Fark.com domain name for a vanity site, so I decided to wait until I had a better idea.

A year and a half later, in February of 1999, I had two ideas. One was to build an Indian curry recipe database. There's still only one good curry database on the Internet, Death By Curry. I still haven't gotten around to doing this one; maybe someday I'll get back to it. The other idea was to do what Fark eventually became. Phil had gotten an e-mail account, as had a few of my other friends, and I was sending them strange news articles multiple times a day. I started to suspect that getting so many e-mails might be really annoying, so I told my friends that I wasn't going to send out e-mails anymore, and that I was going to put them up on Fark.com instead.

I remember sitting in my living room thinking long and hard about starting Fark. I decided if I was going to do it, I would have to do it every single day. I took a deep breath and jumped in.

My friends evidently told other people about Fark. And that's how it all started.

The first year we received 50,000 page views. I was blown away; not a bad number for a site started from scratch. The second year it was a million. Fark's traffic growth has been gradual since it began and there wasn't any one huge hit that made us big. We received some help from TechTV, who had me do a weekly spot on their Screen Savers show via Webcam for about a year and a half. On a week where I did the show, traffic would rise slightly. When I didn't go on the show, it was flat.

From very early on, morning radio shows used Fark as a resource to cull their morning news. A longtime Farker and radio DJ sent me a copy of an internal memo from Clear Channel recommending to all DJs that they use Fark as a resource for show prep. Not surprisingly, a lot of show prep services ("a lot" being "all of them" as far as I can tell) use Fark as a resource as well.

The first year I ran my ISP, our office was in the same building as a radio station. Occasionally I would get up around 5:00 A.M., give up trying to sleep, and go into work early. (I'm genetically a morning person, I just can't help it.) Anyhow, the station's morning DJ, Keith West, who incidentally is still on the air somewhere (hi, Keith), was also at work that early. I got into the habit of joining him in the early mornings just for the company.

Every morning, Keith would arrive at the station an hour before going on air. He would have a copy of every local newspaper, *USA Today,* and a pair of scissors. He would then read all of the newspapers, find material he wanted to discuss, cut the articles out, and organize them for later when he was on air.

I ran into Keith again a couple of years ago. He told me that now instead of one hour before airtime, he arrives about five minutes before he goes on air, pulls up Fark.com, and starts reading it top to bottom. He prints the articles he likes and talks about those during his show. He loves Fark because it gives him an extra hour of sleep each day.

Initially, radio DJs went out of their way to not mention us. As time went on, most discovered that saying they got their stories from Fark didn't hurt them at all. They came to discover that no one cares where radio DJs get their material, they just like hearing it. I actually don't have a problem with radio shows using Fark headlines as long as they can help us out by giving us a mention once in a while. It's great publicity and gets us new readers, which helps tremendously.

One interesting thing about Fark is how many Mass Media people comb Fark for story ideas, not just for radio but for television, newspapers, and Internet media outfits. Once we switched to Google Analytics for Web traffic tracking, we discovered that the number one highest-traffic corporate Internet hitting our servers was CNN. Number two: Fox News. Mass Media even submits a lot of their own articles to Fark, sometimes with taglines so outrageous it's hard to believe these are the same people who run Mass Media. I can't even give any examples; it would be too easy to track back to the source and get people in trouble. The most I can tell you is that it happens multiple times every day. And we really appreciate it.

MASS MEDIA PATTERNS

I've met the guys over at The Smoking Gun (thesmokinggun .com) many, many times. For those few readers out there who are not familiar with The Smoking Gun, they're essentially an investigative journalism Web site. Unlike your average Weblog, The Smoking Gun researches and produces all of their own material. It's usually crime-related but not always. They're not very interested in the media spotlight; in fact they once told me that whenever they get a call from TV media to do an appearance, they fight over who has to do it. It's not that they are introverts, they're definitely not. None of them prefers being in the spotlight, even though the bits I've seen each of them do in the past are top-notch. After having done a bit of TV and radio myself in recent years, I have the occasional flash of clarity in which I completely agree with their feelings about doing Mass Media appearances. It's a fairly demanding prospect, but it's something no one wants to hear about because at the end of the day it's not work, it's just talking with a camera and/or microphone on. The real challenge is not looking like an idiot. It's very easy to look like an idiot.

Because the guys who work on The Smoking Gun are rarely in the public eye, people are curious as to what kind of guys they are. I respond that they're actually doing what every person who ever wanted to be a journalist imagines that the profession is like. They are highly motivated individuals working on cases that are sometimes meaningful, often important, and almost always amusing. They're doing their job well and they are making a difference.

For an example of their tenacity, during one visit I had the opportunity to watch the site founder, Bill Bastone, call Ticketmaster's help line in an attempt to recover some Springsteen tickets that had been lost because of a Web site snafu. He had reserved the tickets he wanted but a click or two later the system released them, and he couldn't find any tickets that were better or even as good. I watched him work his way through their help desk system, being extremely firm and resolved without being the least bit personally insulting. I never did find out if he got the tickets he wanted (it would surprise me to find out he didn't), but what I did find out is that under no circumstances do I ever want the guys at The Smoking Gun coming after me for anything. I've told them this; they tell me that the minute I do something embarrassing they will nail me to the wall. They laugh when they say it (and so do I), but I'm sure they're not kidding.

I point this out because in real life, being a journalist sucks. The pay is horrible, the pressure is high, and journalists spend the vast majority (if not all) of their time just filling space. Part of the problem is that the nature of news has changed. Nowadays, unless you work for a major national media outlet, all of the news is prepackaged by the Associated Press (AP), Reuters, or another wire service.

I'm no journalist, but after reading nearly 2,000 news articles a day since 1999 while running Fark, I've noticed some patterns in the Not News articles that Mass Media consistently likes to run. I've made a list of the most common types of articles that I see, and every day dozens of examples of these media patterns are submitted by our readership. This book will shed some light on these patterns that have been influencing our daily news for years.

It's interesting to note that during times when real news is actually occurring, these types of articles all but disappear from Mass Media. I don't know whether that's disappointing or reassuring.

Incidentally, one of the more surprising things I discovered while researching the articles for this book is that a number of them exactly mirrored a Wikipedia entry on the same subject. I didn't find any exact copies of Wikipedia in the articles in this book, but the structure often was the same and used the same citations in the same places. If I had to guess, I'd say that half of all the "original" articles covered in this book are Wikipedia entry rewrites. If not more. It certainly makes me wonder about the rest of the articles I didn't research. Perhaps that's how the Wikipedia articles were generated in the first place. Due to the obscurity of certain details in some of the articles, and the fact that none of those details showed up in a Google search on the same subject, I am more inclined to believe reporters borrow heavily from Wikipedia, and not the other way around.

I'm being intentionally vague here so no one sues me for all I'm worth. Someone else is welcome to do the follow-up evidence.

Without further ado, here are the patterns around which the book is organized.

Media Fearmongering

Media loves to extrapolate, especially regarding natural disasters. The general question of any fearmongering article is What Would Happen If Some Wildly Improbable Event Occurred? The general answer is: Millions of people would die and civilization as we know it would collapse.

On the morning of the first space shuttle landing since the *Columbia* disaster, I was sitting in the CNN studios in New York waiting to go on. I'd prepared a short three-minute rant on the space shuttle coverage, but I was bumped when the shuttle landing was delayed for twenty-four hours. CNN decided that it was probably not a good idea to have me on to deliver a humorous critique of media coverage of the space shuttle landing before they were done covering it. In retrospect, that was probably a good idea, because media coverage of that first space shuttle landing in two years was embarrassing. If you ran a search on CNN.com for "space shuttle" around that time, literally every article was about the space shuttle blowing up.

Incidentally the ratings for that particular shuttle launch were the highest of any shuttle launch ever. Why? Because everyone tuned in to see if it would explode. Seriously. It was like watching NASCAR race highlights consist of just the wrecks. Incidentally, space shuttle mission coverage is still like this today.

The most over-the-top article was about the potential destruction if (1) something went wrong, (2) the shuttle had to land in the desert, and (3) the shuttle overshot the landing and hit Los Angeles. That's a lot of ifs. Classic fearmongering at its best.

Unpaid Placement Masquerading as Actual Article

A main source of easy-to-write articles is the press release. Every day hundreds of scientific organizations, political think tanks, activist groups, and corporations release scads of press releases about anything under the sun. Most of these are boring as hell, which is often done on purpose, especially when there is bad news to report. The worse the news, the later in the week it is announced. In fact most White House pressrooms (no matter which political party is in charge) toss out a huge dump of bad news around 5:00 P.M. every Friday. Which as far as I can tell is at least five hours after the media corps has clocked out for a three-martini lunch with no intention of coming back to work till Monday.

One tame example of an Unpaid Placement Masquerading as Actual Article is a recent study that indicates that 90 percent of the ocean's large fish species are now extinct. The press release fails to mention how this number was actually determined. It certainly seems plausible that there might be fewer large fish today than in years past. But does the person doing the study know how many large fish species there used to be? Do they know how many there are now? Did someone get out there and count them individually? No. No one knows the current population of all the large fish in the sea. I can't prove it, but even if they did a study, it looks like they just made this up. They get away with this mainly because there's no way to confirm or deny its veracity, but there certainly is no way they could actually know for sure.

At any rate, it turns out that the guy who released this so-called study was promoting a book about damage to the environment. The entire article was effectively an ad for it, thanks to Mass Media giving it some publicity.

Many odd news items are commercials in disguise. They're not necessarily bought and paid for, in payola-type situations, but it's obvious what the point is. Mass Media has been full of these types of articles for years, although most people haven't noticed.

Headline Contradicted by Actual Article

Journalists are taught to sell a story. They hype its conclusions, misconstrue study findings, take things out of context, and generally do whatever it takes to catch your eye to get you to read a story. Occasionally they go too far.

The *Detroit Free Press* ran an article entitled "Asian Vehicles Rank Low in Survey," a headline that appears to state that foreign cars have reliability problems. However, hidden a few paragraphs down was this gem: "But Asian nameplates still dominated the most-reliable list. Of the 31 cars that earned a top reliability rating, 29 were Japanese." Buh?

I've been told by some of my friends in Mass Media that oftentimes the culprit is bad editing or, more to the point, an idiot editor.

Equal Time for Nutjobs

Journalists are taught to give equal time to both sides of a story. Equal time is a great idea when we're talking about debatable issues like school vouchers, immigration reform, and whether or not Duke sucks. There are two sides to all of those arguments (well, except for maybe the "Duke sucks" one). But in some cases, there flat-out isn't another side. Take moon landings, for example. Any time moon landings are mentioned in the media they always have to go get a paragraph of comment from the nutjobs who think the moon landing was faked. This is not up for debate; the moon landings happened. Equal Time for Nutjobs is the kind of article that gives equal time to a group that doesn't deserve to have its voice heard.

The Out-of-Context Celebrity Comment

Usually these celebrity comments are snippets of much larger interviews. The interviewer runs out of "pertinent" questions for the celebrity (How's the movie going? Who are you humping? etc.), so they start asking random questions about the celebrity's personal opinions on things. I can only guess that this is some kind of phishing technique, whereby dozens of questions are asked about unrelated topics in the hope that the celebrity will slip up and say something stupid. Which inevitably happens. Once it does, this stupid statement becomes the story lead.

During the 2004 presidential campaign, political issues seemed to be the hot-button topic. This was probably because the candidates themselves certainly weren't giving any definitive answers. Brad Pitt was asked his position on stem cell research (he liked it). The Dixie Chicks commented on President Bush's foreign policy (they didn't like it). Sean Penn probably did the best of all, voicing his opinion on the state of the Iraq war (didn't like it, but didn't know where Iraq was either). Soon after, Penn was actually picked up as a columnist for the *Los Angeles Times* and sent overseas to Iraq to do some on-the-spot reporting for the newspaper. While there he reportedly punched the hell out of Geraldo Rivera's cameraman, who at the time was not actually in Iraq at all. Which begs the question: Where the hell was Sean

Penn exactly? I won't attempt to answer that one. It turns out that Sean Penn didn't punch anyone, which is as surprising to me as it probably is to you.

Seasonal Articles

As we've mentioned before, when nothing newsworthy is going on, the media is forced to fill column inches with whatever else it can find. There are several seasonal topics the media loves to focus on, articles covered every single year no matter what. The main reason for these repeat articles is twofold. The first reason is that certain publicity-seeking organizations have discovered that if they issue a press release at the same time on the same subject every year, but disguise it as an update of some kind over last year, it will see print every time. The single best example of this is the AAA (or just the plain AA in Britain—not the drunks, the car people). Every single holiday, every local AAA chapter contacts their local Mass Media outlets to notify them that traffic will be bad. Here's a concept: Why not tell us when traffic *won't* be bad? That would be some serious news right there. We already know we're going to hit traffic on Memorial Day, Thanksgiving, Christmas, and all those other holidays. The AAA knows that Mass Media will run it, so they send out the same damn thing every holiday.

Which brings us to the second reason many of these articles repeat every year: Mass Media doesn't like to work during holidays. But newspapers still go out and broadcasters still need material, so why not fill space with articles that you can just keep in a drawer somewhere until you need them? ABC News has a canned bit on how champagne bubbles are caused by dust in the glass. I've seen that at least twice and both times were on New Year's Eve. They probably run it every year, for all I know.

It's not just holidays, though, for just about anything that happens on a seasonal basis has its own seasonal article.

Media Fatigue

Mass Media has a short attention span. If you ask Mass Media people about it, they'll claim it's due to the fact that their readers have a short attention span. That's only part of the story. The other part has to do with the nature of news. It's not possible to run a media outlet repeating the same information over and over again, day in and day out. Unless you are CNN Headline News, and even then it's difficult.

The challenge of reporting is to continually come up with new information on the issues on which you're reporting. This can be extremely difficult if not impossible when dealing with sudden emergencies. Most terrorist attacks fit this pattern. Initially, the media is blindsided by the event. Eyewitness reports start coming in, the vast majority of which are inaccurate. Media outlets don't have the option to remain silent about breaking news, so having nothing else to talk about, they repeat the rumors. Unfortunately, they either don't realize that people take rumor information as fact from mainstream news outlets, or they do realize it but feel they have plausible deniability by reporting rumors as rumor rather than fact.

As minutes and hours pass, rumors are dispelled and real information comes in. Toward the end of a twenty-four-hour period the media usually has a pretty good handle on what actually happened.

Having no new information to report is the bane of Mass Media. As mentioned before, you can't just repeat the same story over and over again, you have to find new information. The only alternative to this is switching to a different story, so if you want to continue to report on something, you've got to start exploring Other Angles.

The first angle covered is interviewing eyewitnesses, as many as possible. These people are usually survivors of some sort of horrible trauma, and too often the media forgets this. Right after Hurricane Katrina hit New Orleans, a Fox News reporter on a live feed interviewed the first person he saw: a man walking a dog.

REPORTER: You're live on Fox News Channel. What are you doing?

MAN (INCREDULOUS): Walking a dog.

REPORTER: Wh-why are you still here? I'm-I'm just curious.

MAN (SLIGHT STUNNED PAUSE): None of your fucking business!

REPORTER: Oh, that was a good answer, wasn't it? That was live on air on national television; thanks so much for that.

MAN: Well, you know . . . (continues yelling at the reporter) [National desk cuts live audio feed]

Media will ask survivors some of the most deplorable questions, such as "How do you feel right now?" "Has this changed your life?" and "Do you think you'll be able to recover and move on?" For most people following these events, the answers are always "Like shit," "Yes," and "Hell no." Although occasionally you'll get people praising and/or crediting Jesus/Muhammad/Buddha/Hubbard-Xenu that they pulled through, conveniently forgetting about the masses of people hurt, maimed, killed, or in the very least not protected by their deity of choice. At any rate it's not the interviewee's fault for coming up with stupid answers. Reporters shouldn't be asking these types of questions in the first place. Just leave the poor bastards alone.

Once the Mass Media has run out of eyewitnesses to interview, they bring in The Experts. The industry refers to them as talking heads, which is the best description of what they actually do: not a goddamn thing. These folks are brought in to kill time while the anchors go on smoke breaks. Occasionally they do offer good insight. However, most of these people aren't currently working in their area of expertise, having quit their day jobs to move on to full-time media expertism.

The final stage is: Has the Media Gone Too Far? This cry goes out once the media has truly run out of things to talk about. They switch focus to examining their own coverage of the event and critiquing whether they went overboard, usually either by covering inane material or by overhyping minutiae. The vast majority of these articles leave the conclusion open-ended, but the real answer to Has the Media Gone Too Far? is yes, it goddamn very well has. And you can bet the farm that they'll do the exact same thing next time around.

This cycle lasts two or three days on major media events (kids falling down wells, pop stars being acquitted, space shuttles exploding), and lasts as little as twenty-four hours on more minor stories (politician extramarital affairs, streakers at sporting events, controversial music/TV/radio). Once the cycle is complete, coverage of the initial event drops off to nothing. The media will have exhausted every potential angle on the story and needs to move on. This is Media Fatigue.

The longest we've ever seen a cycle go without repeating is a week. Only two news events have ever done this. One was 9/11. The other was Janet Jackson's boob popping out at the Super Bowl. Yeah.

Lesser Media Space Fillers

For whatever reason, Mass Media feels compelled to consistently write about certain topics. These are not tied to any particular part of the calendar year, they are articles that Mass Media simply can't resist publishing whenever they occur. These include missing white chicks, plane crashes, and amputations of random body parts.

Using some of the best stories from Fark as examples, let's examine how these media patterns apply. You may notice that some of the article headlines seem a little strange. That's because they are the taglines that appeared on Fark and not the actual headlines of the articles themselves. The comments that follow each article (with spelling and punctuation as in the originals) are the postings from Fark's discussion board at the time the original article came out.

Media Fearmongering

"Can a common household object kill you and everyone you know? Find out after this break."
—LOCAL TV ANCHORWOMAN ON ANY GIVEN NIGHT IN AMERICA

ON THE MORNING THAT KATRINA HIT NEW ORLEANS, I WAS IN New York to do a spot on CNN. I ended up getting bumped because apparently a story about a hurricane destroying a major U.S. city rates higher than the goofy crap we cover on Fark. Fair enough. In the middle of major disasters, people really don't want to hear about people getting their wangs cut off by ex-girlfriends, or tractor trailer accidents that spilled food all over major U.S. highways. Actual news is going on, a rarity, unfortunately. Or fortunately, depending on how you look at it.

After CNN I was scheduled to be on Opie and Anthony on XM Radio. What was supposed to be a fifteen-minute segment stretched into an hour and a half as we discussed all the permutations of the Katrina situation. One of the bits I did for the show was to compile all of the worst-case scenarios that had appeared in Mass Media and merge them into one huge Worst-Case Scenario. It turns out that if you lived in New Orleans during Katrina and every bad thing the media predicted actually came to pass, you'd find yourself in a tree because the entire city would be under ten feet of water. You would also be under attack by balls of fire ants atop floating coffins that would be everywhere. Additionally, the river would be on fire.

The Mississippi River would catch fire because nearby petroleum refineries would be flooded and then somehow explode (which seems kind of contradictory to me). As far as the fire ants go, it turns out they can actually cross rivers. They lump themselves into a large ball and spin themselves across bodies of water. The floating coffins would have surfaced because no one in New Orleans is buried above sea level. There were actual articles devoted to all of these subjects.

It was hilarious. At the time. However, by the end of the day, New Orleans was indeed destroyed. While I didn't read anything about flaming coffins containing balls of fire ants, a good chunk of the city did end up underwater. We kind of looked like idiots for making fun of the destruction of New Orleans on the radio as it was happening. Therein lies the problem of making fun of Media Fearmongering: If the disaster actually happens, you are an idiot. A shortsighted idiot who didn't see the writing on the wall that was plain as day to everyone else. Even though no one else really believed it could happen at the time.

People are hindsighted. Everyone generally agrees, for example, that the dot-com boom of the late 1990s was a bunch of over-hyped crap. At the time no one believed it, though. Fark started back in 1999. One of my pet peeves at the time was people who bought into the dot-com bubble. We made a point of posting articles highlighting this stupidity whenever possible, kind of the same way we like to highlight the fact that Duke sucks. Nowadays you can't find anyone in the news media who will admit to thinking at the time that the dot-com boom was legitimate. Everyone saw it coming, according to their own accounts anyhow.

This chapter pokes fun at such overhyped media garbage. On the off chance any of it does happen, just remember you didn't see it coming either. Let's kick this off with a subject near and dear to my heart, literally.

THERE'S A SEISMIC FAULT LINE IN THE MIDWEST. <u>EVERYBODY PANIC</u>.

When I was six or seven years old I felt my first earthquake. I was with my mom and grandmother in our kitchen at the time. It was a long, low rumble that went on for quite a while. We didn't know what it was because we were in central Kentucky, and an earthquake was the last thing we expected.

It turns out that there's a huge fault line that runs roughly along the Mississippi River. It stretches from south of the place where the Missouri, Illinois, and Kentucky borders all meet, to north of where Arkansas, Missouri, and Tennessee intersect. They call it the New Madrid Fault, named after the town pretty much at the center of the fault line in Missouri that will be completely and utterly destroyed if the fault ever pops.

The New Madrid Fault is inactive most of the time. Every few years it tosses out a 3.0 or so, everyone talks about it for twenty-four hours, then forgets about it again. Discussion of these shocks tend to irritate Californians, who scoff at the media coverage, since they are so accustomed to quakes that they don't feel anything less than a 4.0. The quake from my childhood didn't cause much damage at all. I remember going to the store soon after and aisle 5 had suffered a few casualties in the form of pickle jars that had fallen off the shelves. That was about it for damage. Suffice it to say we watched the news that night for some great earthquake damage video and saw the same pickles in the footage. Poor pickles.

The problem with the New Madrid Fault is that usually it doesn't do much, but occasionally it pops big. Occasionally being once every few hundred years. Between 1811 and 1812 several massive tremors issued from the New Madrid Fault; their relative strength is estimated at between 7.7 and 9.2, depending on who you ask. No one really knows because very few people lived in the area at the time, and those people who did live there weren't taking seismic readings. Every account I've ever read says that the Mississippi River flowed backward for a while and that the quake was so strong that it rang church bells in Baltimore/New York/Boston, depending on which account you read. Everyone always mentions the church bells. You'd think that if it were strong enough to ring church bells a thousand miles away, there would have been some other exceptional damage to the city, but no one mentions anything. Aside from those large quakes, there were a few other strong quakes during the nineteenth century. But then in the twentieth century, nothing. This is where the Media Fearmongering comes into play. We're "overdue" for a big one.

Most people outside of the Midwest and South Central U.S. have never heard of the New Madrid Fault. Those of us who live within three hundred miles of it, however, are well aware. The media won't let us forget it.

When I was a senior in high school, some nutjob claiming to be able to predict earthquakes said that there was going to be a huge earthquake in December 1990. New Madrid was jam-packed with national media, satellite trucks, and anchor wannabees who apparently just couldn't wait to throw themselves into the epicenter of possibly the worst earthquake in U.S. history. The reason I can remember when this happened is because there was a rumor going around at the time that the Big One would happen on 12/3 at 4:56 P.M. It would be a 7.8 earthquake. In '90. 1234567890. Which as far as I can tell is exactly how this genius deduced the time himself, because jack shit happened. A week of media hoopla generated for nothing. Most of the high school stayed home that day just in case. High school kids will skip school for any semi-plausible reason. As of this writing, earthquake drills are still run in Kentucky public schools on a regular basis.

The specific article about the New Madrid fault posted to Fark came in on the hundredth anniversary of the San Francisco quake. Not much was going on other than that, so it was time for some conjecture. Besides, the New Madrid Will Kill Us All articles hadn't been run in a while, so out it came. According to the article, 11 million people live in the quake zone now, as opposed to four hundred people back in 1811. Memphis and St. Louis are at extreme risk because there are no earthquake-proofing regulations in their zoning laws. For some reason Louisville always gets left out, probably because they don't have a pro sports team or something. I've spent a lot of time in downtown Louisville, and I'm no expert on architecture, but it's not too much of a leap of faith to say they're completely screwed if the Big One hits. Most of the article actually consisted of talking about other huge earthquakes in other areas because there just hasn't been one at the New Madrid Fault.

And I should point out here that while I'm making fun of Mass Media over the New Madrid Fault coverage, if I ever build a house, I'm planning on earthquake-proofing it. Because, why not?

» Soze

Well, there are lots of dairy farms in the Midwest, and I like milkshakes, so I see no problems with this. Also, all of our meat and pork will come pre-tenderized.

So really, the question is why aren't we packing this fault with dynamite already?

» Bluegill

We had a quake here in Southwest Ohio about the time that The Empire Strikes Back was released. I was pissed because I missed the quake. I didn't notice it, because I was in the movie theater at the time watching the movie.

» KentuckyBob

Every 4 years some hippie reporter brings this old story back up, hoping to be the one who broke this story.

   Congrats Marsha Walton of CNN.com you are this year's boob.

» Shostie

Fools. Everyone knows that earthquakes are the result of
Zeus' anger.

» Comfortably_dumb

Is it just me, or does everyone here seem to think the "midwest" is everything that isn't NY or CA?

» Snarfangel

Can't we use our earthquake generator to divert it to some place uninhabited, like Canada?

SCIENTISTS FROM LA JOLLA ALL THE WAY TO PISMO SAY THE SAN ANDREAS FAULT IS "WAITING TO EXPLODE."

I have a theory, based on some anecdotal evidence that I can't really back up, that most of the California Is Doomed stories come out during the summer, when there isn't much going on. Slow news day? Run the one about earthquakes in California. Or wildfires. Or volcanoes. Or tsunamis. Or David Hasselhoff.

The actual headline of the article is "Southern San Andreas Fault Waiting to Explode." Yup, just sitting around waiting. Until no one's looking. Then it will hop out from behind a bush and KILL US ALL EVERYBODY PANIC.

"The southern end of the San Andreas Fault near Los Angeles, which has been still for more than two centuries, is under immense stress and could produce a massive earthquake at any moment, a scientist said on Wednesday." You have to wonder whether or not the guy lost a bet. I'd hate to be the guy who has to stand up at a press conference and state the obvious over and over again. In true journalistic form, after stating the scary premise, the article must now tell us why we suddenly have to care about earthquakes in California, which as far as everyone else is concerned, especially Californians, are damn near ubiquitous.

"'The observed strain rates confirm that the southern section of the San Andreas Fault may be approaching the end of the interseismic phase of the earthquake cycle,' Yuri Fialko wrote in the science journal *Nature*."

Oh no! Uh. Whatever that means.

Then comes my favorite almost–non sequitur of the article: "A sudden lateral movement of 7 to 10 meters would be among the largest ever recorded." Well, no shit. No word if he actually ever said that. The article might as well have said, "If my aunt had balls she'd be my uncle." Yes, indeed she would.

The short version of the rest of the article is that the tectonic plates of San Andreas have been slipping elsewhere a few centimeters a year, but not in Los Angeles. So there you have it, California is doomed. Later, guys.

» Wmoonfox

Far too many reporters watched that History Channel special last night.

» Honeyporter

My headline would have been "I guess we haven't had enough shark attacks this summer . . ."

» Weazelbeater

Welcome to Arizona Bay.

» L33t Squirrel

I like the sound of "The Gulf of Nevada" myself.

» Elburrittobandito

I wonder if, when the big one hits, people will have the same condescending attitude towards dead/displaced Angelenos that they had towards Katrina victims. You know, the "That's what you get for building a city in a swamp" theory.

I will be condescending, just wondering about the rest of you.

» GWSuperfan

The San Andreas is a strike-slip fault. That means that the stuff to the west on the Pacific Plate (L.A.) moves north relative to the stuff on the North American plate. L.A. will wind up as a suburb of San Francisco, not fall off into the ocean.

» Palin88

Haha, I'm right with ya, living in Arroyo Grande. Earthquakes and exploding power plants and breaking dams don't scare me. For some reason though, I'm terrified at the thought of tornadoes. I guess it just depends on where you grew up. You Kansas people just keep those whirling death funnels away from me, and I'll enjoy the nice massage I get from the magnitude 5 earthquake bouncing my house.

OH MY GOD, THERE'S BACTERIA ON EVERYTHING.

One of the staples of Media Fearmongering is the Bacteria Is Found Everywhere article. This oftentimes assumes the form of articles about elementary school kids taking swabs from ordinary household surfaces and growing them in petri dishes. For all I know, this is a part of nearly ever kid's science curriculum; hell, we even did it when I was a kid.

Usually these articles take one of two tacks. The first is that one of the kids inevitably grabs a swab from the school toilet. This is held up by Mass Media as the Worst Possible Outcome sample, in that any petri dish that grows bacteria worse than what you find on the inside of a toilet is Really Bad. As it turns out, urine is sterile and toilets are cleaned with bleach, so there are quite a lot of things that have more bacteria on them than the inside of a toilet. Just about anything, actually.

The second tack the media takes is noting the absolute worst thing the kids find in their petri dish experiments. This is almost always a common household object. If you think about it, this makes sense. If people weren't touching the damn things so often, there wouldn't be any bacteria on them at all. Bacteria aren't immortal; it can't live forever outside of the human body. Well, most can't. In recent years, two things usually get mentioned as the most bacteria-ridden objects: cash money and computer keyboards.

How this gets into the Mass Media over and over and over and over is anyone's guess. Most likely it comes from the bottom up, in that it's picked up by local news first, then rolls from there. Local news gets it because people at the local TV station or newspaper have kids that are doing these experiments and they remember that editorial will damn near always run one of these stories. The fearmongering bacteria articles tend to space themselves out, mainly because it butts up against the regular media cycle, in particular the part about the media not being able to run a second story about a situation that has not changed. They have to wait until everyone has forgotten before running it again.

These stories are particularly silly because there isn't anything to worry about. Yes, there are a lot of bacteria on household objects. They rarely kill anyone. You can tell by the lack of general warnings we've been given about not touching money or not using our keyboards for fear of killing ourselves.

Very rarely the media will come up with a few variations on this theme. But there are exceptions....

Tests show shopping-cart handles and mice at Internet cafes are the most bacteria-ridden public items.

This particular article wasn't instigated by kids. Clorox sponsored this study. The article claims that Clorox purportedly sponsored the study to find the places containing the most bacteria in your daily life. So this article also qualifies as an Unpaid Placement Masquerading as Actual Article, but the Media Fearmongering component is much stronger.

The study concluded that teachers', accountants', and bankers' offices harbored "2 to 20 times more bacteria per square inch than other professions." The number one place for bacteria to hide? Phones, actually. Desks came in second, followed by keyboards and mice. Seems kind of unfair to rank all those objects together considering they're usually sitting right next to each other, reinfecting themselves over and over (as far as I know). The lead researcher in the study blamed people eating at their desks for feeding the bacteria farms. Sure, that sounds plausible.

The article also goes on to point out that there are 265 times more bacteria on keyboards than on toilet seats. Yup, they went right for the toilet comparison.

What the article doesn't say is what kind of bacteria was found. Most bacteria are harmless. I suspect this fact wasn't mentioned because the study was more interested in proving that there's a lot of bacteria in general and to remind you that Clorox can take care of that for you. The lead researcher actually recommended using disinfectant wipes to clean your office areas. Guess which company makes those. Yeah.

» Bake2

They have antibacterial wipes at the supermarkets to wipe the shopping cart handles. This is good for those OCD people who are afraid of germs around every corner, bad for the rest of us who have to deal with drug resistant bacterium.

» Daniels

Someone just recently started marketing little knitted wraps for shopping cart handles. True story, when I was working in the supermarket one time I saw a woman who had the handle of the cart all wrapped up, but had her kid in one of the attached cart seats without anything between him and the funk . . . AND he was chewing on the belt. Things like that made my stay there worthwhile. That and the naked goodness I'd occasionally get when developing photos.

I ride the NYC subway every day, I think I'm officially resistant to the plague now.

Girl's science-fair project reveals that the ice served by local fast-food restaurants has more bacteria than their toilets.

You'll note we're sticking with the theme of kids doing science experiments. Again, who else would be doing them? In this case, a Tampa middle schooler decided to test the bacteria content from samples of restaurant ice from five different central Florida fast-food joints. Not surprisingly, she found bacteria in the ice and compared the samples to a toilet water sample. Also not surprisingly, the toilet water was cleaner than 70 percent of the samples she took.

University of South Florida professor Daniel Lim pointed out in a *USA Today* article on the subject that we should "keep in mind, the source of the toilet water is the same as the ice. Toilets are routinely flushed, so you probably don't have many bacteria." He also added that the ice could have come into contact with the bacteria from its containers or handlers. And besides, they scrub the hell out of those fast-food-restaurant toilets, often hourly.

But here comes the interesting twist: Three of the five ice samples tested positive for fecal coliform bacteria. Otherwise known as E. coli. That's some seriously bad shit right there, literally. But wait, in the same article Lim notes that it takes a lot more E. coli to cause disease than was found. Yes, there's an allowable amount of E. coli in food. It's best not to think about it.

In MSNBC's article, the following bit of information appeared: "Galina Tuninskaya, vice president of Applied Consumer Services, a private lab that tests drinking water, said the standard for drinking water is usually 100 colony-forming units of bacteria per milliliter. The highest amount Jasmine found was 54 units in ice from a self-serve machine."

So in conclusion, we're screwed. At least as far as allowable quantities of E. coli in food goes. There's just no way to live in a vacuum, folks. The upshot here is that none of these restaurants had a health problem as far as regulatory guidelines were concerned, but they still had to suffer through a round of media coverage claiming their toilets were cleaner then their ice machines. Because they were. It just wasn't a health problem.

» Jeremyrainman

Yeah, but given the choice between toilet cooties and ice-bucket cooties . . .

» Cadderpidder

Just make ice out of the toilet water. Problem solved!

» ZAZ

There's a reason your dog drinks out of the toilet bowl instead of the icemaker.

» Inthe8Os

Of course people tend to use bleach on their toilets, which they tend to avoid using in their ice cubes.

» BlindMan

Ask yourself:

1) Have you ever eaten fast food?
2) Are you currently dead or suffering from a debilitating condition?

If you answered 1) yes and 2) no, calm the fark down.

» EdgeRunner

If toilet seats are the cleanest surfaces on Earth, it must be because we're always buffing them with our bottoms. So for your safety, rub all food against your barenaked ass before eating.

But wait till I've got the webcam set up.

» Ronaprhys

for those of you faulting the girl, remember that she's in 7th grade. For her, this is good science—at least she tested and proved something.

For the reporter, it's a case of bad science.

» HellYeahHokie

Deaths from fecal bacteria exposure are statistically non-existent (in the United States). They are on the order of 0-15 per year. To put that in perspective, there are about 20,000 deaths per year from the common flu. (numbers from the Center for Disease Control)

The only reason this gets news is because of the icky factor.

TERRORISTS ARE EVERYWHERE.

Ever since 9/11, it's almost as if the media has been on a single-minded mission to elucidate every single possible way in which terrorists can kill us. Back in 2002 I read an interesting article about memos found on confiscated Al Qaida computers in Afghanistan. Apparently they were having a discussion about trying to obtain biological weapons, something they hadn't ever considered until (and it said this in the memos) they read in Mass Media how easy it was to obtain biological weapons. They'd had no idea until they read it in the news. Thanks, Mass Media. Amusingly, in those same memos were details of a long, drawn-out series of interactions be-tweein Al Qaida and the Russian Mafia to purchase a nuclear weapon. Apparently the Russian Mafia claimed they had a nuclear weapon, but every time Al Qaida made a payment, the Russian Mafia would send over a truckload of Volkswagen parts and broken refrigerators. The computers were confiscated while Al Qaida was in the middle of an internal conversation about whether or not, if they sent money to the Russian Mafia for the third time, there was any chance they'd get their nuke. Some members of Al Qaida were beginning to suspect that the Russian Mafia was just keeping their money and had no intentions of shipping them a nuclear weapon.

Nuclear weapons aren't the only things terrorists can buy. If they lower their expectations they can start out with one of these babies:

Although SA-7s and their variants have been around for almost thirty-five years, ABC says now is the time to panic over one of them shooting down the airplane you're on.

First, the media outrage: "But U.S. commercial aircraft still have no defense system against these portable missiles." ABC informs us that shoulder-fired missiles can be obtained for a few thousand dollars on the black market. They're also responsible for twenty-four civilian aircraft having been shot down. In the world.

Note the use of the term *civilian aircraft*. It doesn't say "passenger jet." If you do the quick math using one of the other stats in the story (500 total deaths), you'll note that there's a fatality rate of about twenty people per aircraft getting shot down at the rate of about one aircraft every two and a half years. Eight people per year. Yeah, let's spend millions of dollars to protect eight people per year, even though it's never happened in the U.S. before. Great idea. While we're at it, let's spend billions of dollars making sure people don't take forks on airplanes. Oh, wait.

The article describes a situation in Los Angeles where a commercial jetliner reported seeing a plume of smoke that could have been a rocket, but nothing happened and no one ever found out what it was. EVERYBODY PANIC. They go on to talk about how Israel has missile countermeasures installed on airplanes, but I'm willing to bet this is because they're surrounded by neighboring countries that try to kill them all the time (and vice versa). You don't see Canada or Mexico trying to invade the United States every decade or so, although some would argue Mexico has been doing it one person at a time for years now.

I once read an interesting article about terrorists using heat-seeking military weapons on the geopolitical intelligence Web site Stratfor.com. It said that the success rate with shoulder-fired heat seekers is extremely low because terrorists are ignorant bastards who don't read instructions and fire the things when the plane is too close. It takes time for a heat-seeking missile to get a lock on a plane, and if it goes past before it gets a lock, the missile just keeps on going. Bet that's hard to explain when they get back to terrorist HQ.

» Weaver95

Someone got their wires crossed—this is "panic about global warming" week—NOT "panic about shoulder launched missiles" week.

» Quick1

When is the next "panic about missing white woman" week? It's been a while.

» Quadruplator

Wasn't the SA-7 in Battlefield Vietnam? You couldn't hit shit with that thing, I wouldn't worry about it.

» HeinousJay

Quoting the article: Worldwide, at least 24 civilian aircraft have been brought down by shoulder-fired missiles, and more than 500 people have been killed.

How many people, in the same period, were killed by coconuts hitting them in the head?

Apparently, 150 a year.

That's more deaths than caused by SA-7 shoulder-mounted rockets fired at passenger planes. Where's the fearmongering about coconuts?

» nosajghoul

More planes have been brought down by foreign object damage (screwdrivers, bolts, rags etc . . .) than by this.

Clearly, its time to eliminate screwdrivers, bolts, and rags etc. . . .

To be fair, Mass Media wasn't generating all of the articles on terrorists blowing stuff up. Sure, the articles about terrorists poisoning dams, planting livestock infected with mad cow disease in slaughterhouses, or flying planes into nuclear plants probably did come straight from the minds of the media. Others, however, came from a different source: politicians. Or to be more specific, government agencies themselves. Once Homeland Security began to receive its billions, I can only imagine that it had to scramble to find things to spend the money on. Such as protecting Kentucky goats from terrorist attacks.

Kentucky officials run terrorism drill at goat show. "We try to focus on what really matters to Kentucky," says Homeland Security Department.

Shelly Whitehead must have had a sense of humor when writing this one for *The Kentucky Post*. To wit:

> The bucolic and seemingly safe setting of a goat show turned into something far more sinister in Erlanger on Tuesday, when about 200 people participated in Kentucky's first statewide agricultural terrorism exercise.

I can't imagine the horror of being a journalist and getting handed this assignment.

Kentucky has way too many Homeland Security dollars. I say this because I live in Kentucky, and given the number of terrorist attacks we've had in my lifetime (zero) and the number of potentially interesting targets for terrorists in Kentucky (zero), Homeland Security money spent here is wasted. The problem lies with government departments—if they have too much money in their budgets, they can't just give it back. Certainly that's how the system is supposed to work, but the problem is, once they voluntarily give back budgeted funds, their annual budget going forward gets cut permanently.

So to prevent this, they damn well better come up with something to spend the money on. Like protecting goats from the terrorists. Homeland Security coordinated a drill in Erlanger, Kentucky, with "80 local, state, and federate agencies."

Homeland Security's explanation for the staged attack: "Kentucky is one of the nation's top five goat-producing states; setting the attack at a goat show seemed plausible." Here's another thing to point out: If they say one of the top five, then it's number five. Because if Kentucky were the number one goat-producing state, they would say that instead. I've lived in Kentucky most of my life and have never seen a goat farm. They're probably around somewhere, but my point is, it likely doesn't take a lot of goats to be the number five goat-producing state.

The concept for the attack was that terrorists would infect a goat with a bio-agent and smuggle it into the goat fair. People would pet the goats, go home, and die horrible painful deaths.

An amusing aside on this one: We linked the story on Fark, which soon ended up on every morning radio show and late-night TV talk show on the planet. A friend of mine works for the Kentucky state government. He received a call soon after we linked the article, asking about his friend (me) that ran that Fark site. They passed along a message: "Thanks a hell of a lot." No doubt the ensuing press conferences over the next few days to answer questions about terrorist goat attacks were a good time.

» MyNameIsMofuga

The people of Kentucky have nothing to worry about unless the terrorists give STDs to the sheep.

» Cupajo

Quoting the article: Kentucky is one of the nation's top five goat-producing states.

Yeah! We finally cracked the top five! Take that, Tennessee!

» Dball2

Ahhhh . . . The Kentucky Office For Homeland Security working feverishly to keep the unwashed masses safe. Gotta love the return we get on Government these days.

I can't even imagine how stupid I'd feel strapping on the tie and walking out the door if I had any involvement in this.

» HotWingConspiracy

Quoting the article: Also, the terrorists could easily launch a suicide attack on the Marble Hill nuclear plant.

Then run a drill addressing that. Or would they somehow attack via goat?

» hoohoodilly

Yeah, everyone complains about what a waste of resources this is. Then, when the terrorists target Kentucky goats, the same people will be screaming, "Why weren't our goats prepared?!"

» nytmare

Terrorists: How can we get America's goat? I know! Quick, Ahmed, get me a list of the top five goat-producing american states.

» Nuclear Monk

Laugh all you want . . . but I remember how I felt when the first goat slammed into the World Trade Center and I WILL NOT FORGET!

THREE FLORIDA WOMEN HAVE BEEN KILLED BY ALLIGATORS IN ONE WEEK. MEDIA HYSTERIA TO BEGIN IN FIVE . . . FOUR . . . THREE . . . TWO . . . ONE . . .

I often get asked where the Florida tag came from on Fark. It kind of stands out, since most of the other tags are adjectives, and Florida is a state.

Back in 2000, you may recall there were some problems with an election in Florida, whatever that was all about. While all that was going on, I started getting multiple requests for a Florida tag. The idea being that so many stupid things happen in Florida, it deserved its own Fark tag. I wasn't convinced it would get much use, but I decided to go ahead and put it up anyhow.

Boy, was I wrong.

The Florida tag gets used many times a day, as it turns out. For some reason, Florida is messed up. I would even go as far to say that part of the problem is that Florida is slightly more organized than Jamaica. Perhaps it's the warm weather that makes people stupid. Perhaps it's the Real World–like population demographic, where old people, Cuban immigrants, gobs of tourists, and rednecks all mix together in one huge melting pot of crap. Perhaps it's because there's nothing else really going on in Florida. Who knows?

Whatever the reason, Florida is without a doubt the number one state for weird news. You'd think California would be at least number two, but so far, from where I sit, the front runners are Ohio and Texas, in that order. California's weird news is pretty one-dimensional. It generally elicits the response "Oh, those crazy hippies" because their weird news generally conforms to that sort of thing. Take, for example, the city of Berkeley passing an ordinance stating that people who owned pets were the pets' guardians, not their owners. Oh, those crazy hippies. See? You can write that off as a lifestyle choice. Hippies are weird because they choose to be, and thus it doesn't quite hit you with that "What the hell are they thinking" vibe when you read about them doing weird stuff. Of course hippies would vote to make people pet guardians instead of pet owners. No one is surprised in the least.

Florida weirdness is much more diverse, and seems to be endemic to the population. The people involved in Florida stories, and this absolutely does include presidential elections, are bona fide hosed up. It's not a lifestyle choice, it's who they are. Although I would be willing to bet that most of it begins with a few beers and goes downhill from there. Consider for a moment how many of the best stories about you and your friends begin with the phrase "this one time we were drinking..." Throw in some old people and some lost tourists and you have a fiesta of weirdness.

Considering how insane the state of Florida is, one thing they do not do is go nuts about gators. Sharks are fair game, though, especially during the late spring and early summer. Florida residents treat gators like California residents treat earthquakes: They ignore them completely. Nothing makes a Floridian madder than people taking pictures of gators. "Stupid tourists," they yell, shaking their fists. I'm not exaggerating. Try it the next time you're in Florida. The locals are the ones shaking their heads in disgust.

That's what makes this article all the stranger. Three gator attacks in a week make for an article that for whatever reason hits the national news media. I'm willing to bet that even this has happened before in Florida. What makes this time so different?

There have been seventeen recorded fatal alligator attacks in fifty years of recordkeeping (talk about a thankless job, Alligator Fatality Statistician). Still, as any stockbroker will tell you, past performance is no indication of future returns. Second, two of the three were young white females. The third was a middle-aged white female. The media absolutely cannot resist anything having to do with hot white chicks in distress. While the gator attacks alone probably didn't warrant news, the added factor of young white chicks pushed it over the top.

This article seeing print unfortunately opened the door for a rash of gator-related articles, including one about a woman who shot a gator that was attacking her dog. This made the news in part because she was cited for illegal hunting.

» Badafuco

Wow, there must not be any shark attacks to report right now.

» Popain

aligators: check
hurricanes: check
high crime: check
old people: check
People live there why?

» Justanotherfarkinfarker

Insainly hot latin women & hot white trash: check
Waffle house on every St.: check
Legal fireworks: check

» Bustedback

Gators don't eat vegetables because the wheelchairs
get in the way.

» No_one_special

For some reason, I seem to have this natural tendency to avoid large,
carnivorous reptiles.
    Must be just me.

» Danploon

I remember when gators were on the endangered species list. I also
remember why.

» Tonmeister

We had a gator in our backyard when I was growing up in Collier County.
The neighbor used to feed it raw meat using a baseball glove as "protection".
That would piss off my dad who knew that once a gator figures out people
equal an easy food source, it wasn't long before the gator got greedy and
would try to bite off a little more. Luckily, we moved a couple years later to a
more "civilized" part of town. These were the same neighbors, of course,
who used to ride their motorbikes on their roof

» Serutan

It's just God punishing Florida for having so much outdoor sex.

U.S. UNABLE TO STOP ACTIVE
BIRD-FLU PANDEMIC

Here's a subject that without a doubt will get me in trouble. There hasn't been a good pandemic in a while, but they used to happen with frightening regularity up until two generations ago. Without a doubt, there is another global pandemic coming. Luckily we can all count on Mass Media to cover every possible angle before any serious threat has even been identified.

Case in point: the bird flu. From a cursory reading of Mass Media, average Joe will conclude two things. (1) The bird flu is highly contagious and (2) it will kill us all. It turns out that it's slightly more complicated than that. While people can catch the bird flu, they generally need to be in close contact with infected birds. It helps to have several infected birds running around the dirt floors of your house, shitting on everything. You also need to roll around in the bird shit on a regular basis. It also helps to be living in a third-world country where medical care sucks donkey balls. Using severed chicken heads as soccer balls or teething rings isn't a bad idea either.

Often lost in the bird flu coverage is the underlying fear that the bird flu, which is not easy to catch from a chicken and as far as we know completely impossible to catch from another human, might merge with a regular old flu virus and become a superbug that will kill us all. Scientists believe this has happened in the past; however, the odds aren't very high of the bird flu specifically going the same route. Most people aren't aware of this, because Bird Flu Will Kill Us All has been a page 1 story ever since the SARS outbreak a few years back was so disappointing from a media standpoint.

An article entitled Bird Flu May Not Be That Dangerous

warrants page 5 or later. No one gets really excited about something being less dangerous than advertised.

This particular article is about a study in the journal *Nature* on what would happen to the United States if a pandemic broke out. Here's the good news: If the United States does nothing, 33 percent of the population will be infected. In my opinion that's pretty damn good. Every year everyone I know gets the flu, usually twice. Once in early winter, once in late winter after you think you're safe because you had the flu in early winter. Everyone gets it. That would be 100 percent for those of you not good at math. We'll call it 99 percent because there's always some jackass who doesn't come down with it, and who feels compelled to remind you of this all year long. Here's the bad news: If the United States tries really hard, it will drop the infection rate from 33 percent to 28 percent. As crappy as that rate of improvement is, that 5 percent represents about 8 million people. The study doesn't say whether they expect any flu precautions made currently by the government to be effective. Personally I wouldn't bet on it.

Just as with the Y2K fiasco, Hollywood eventually got around to making a made-for-TV movie: *Fatal Contact*. The bird flu kills millions of people, whose corpses get piled up and burned. That's pretty much the movie; sorry if I spoiled it for you. Brought to you by the same people that made *Atomic Twister*. Yeah, I didn't see that one either.

» Crosshair
Considering how well we can stop drugs and illegals from getting into the country, this should not come as any surprise.

» Bugs_Bunny_Practiced_Psychological_Warfare
Wait. I forget. Are the terrorists trying to scare everyone or is it the media?

» West_Side_Charlie

From the article: So far this year H5N1 bird flu—which doesn't move
easily from person to person—has infected 204 people and killed 113,
according to the World Health Organization.

. . . moving it past "slipping on banana peels" and "freak peanut allergies"
on the list of top worldwide killers

» Stupid_Flanders

It's the flu. Medicine has progressed quite a bit since 1918. What you can
buy off the shelf at the corner drug store is superior to what hospitals were
dishing out then. We know more about how flu is spread, and how to
manage symptoms.

I'm not scared. Well, I'm scared of clowns. And bears. And midgets and
carneys and banjo players. But that's it.

» Sheila_McSly

I think most of us understand that the threat is real. But when the "conse-
quences" are OH MY GOD CIVILIZATION IS COMING TO AN END, RUN! STOCK-
PILE FOOD AND AMMO! PLANT CORN! you're either going to be miserable and
paranoid or, you know, a little glib. And I've tried miserable paranoia; there's no
future in it. Let me know when it can be passed along with a sneeze, otherwise,
there are a whole lot of better Apocalypses out there to fret about.

» Juniorll

Great. What am I supposed to do with all this bird feces that I bought for the
party this weekend?

» brap

My biggest fear is that I will begin coughing up blood on this tie, which I just
had dry-cleaned.

» Outatime

Does this mean no more pigeon sushi?

» Gosling

So let me get this straight:
*So far, worldwide, there have been about 100 cases spread over many
countries, including ones in which there's really no healthcare or
disease prevention to speak of.

*But the United States, with some of the highest-quality healthcare in the world and many disease-prevention programs, is completely unable to keep the exact same disease from infecting less than 28% of the American populace?

I call bullshit.

Y2K—THE NON-DISASTER

On January 1, 2000, the BBC ran an article summarizing the effects of the much-hyped Y2K bug. In particular they succeeded in getting the following quote:

> "One of the questions you've begun to see surface is, 'well, has this all been hype?'" said John Koskinen, the U.S. Y2K troubleshooter.
>
> The answer is no, he said, adding that preparing for Y2K had been "the biggest management challenge the world has had in 50 years.... I think that we should not underestimate the nature of the problem that was originally there."

Thus proving how difficult it is to admit that the last few years of your life have been a complete and utter waste of time.

People talked about Y2K back when I was in college in the early 1990s. It was one of those problems that "someone" should do "something" about "really soon." However, no one was moving forward on the issue. Kind of like any number of other "going to kill us all" issues that you can think of off the top of your head.

The problem stemmed from legacy code left over from the days when computing power came at a very high price. Computer processing power and disk space (or punch card space, depending on how long ago we're talking) were very expensive commodities. You didn't waste any space if you could help it.

Back in the day, and by this I mean the 1950s and 1960s (if not later), many programmers represented dates as six-digit values. For example, 01/01/51 would mean January 1, 1951. The Y2K problem arose when you could no longer assume that the first two digits of the year value were 19. Using the same example as above, 01/01/00 would mean January 1, 1900. This can be a problem if the year is really 2000.

As the decade went on, the media started jumping up and down about the Y2K bug. It helped that no one really knew what the extent of the problem was; as a result, no one could stand up and effectively argue that there was no problem. It certainly seemed plausible that Y2K might cause problems at the time.

As January 1 neared, Fark linked to some of the more amusing public reactions covered in the media. One of which is hallmark of a disaster that isn't truly a disaster: the made-for-TV movie. In this case, it was entitled *Y2K*. It's literally impossible to find anyone who actually watched this movie. Odds are the main characters spent most of the movie running around yelling "Oh, crap" while stuff blew the hell up. Pretty compelling stuff. And broadcast networks wonder why their ratings are going down.

An article on excite.com wasted our time with an article about how there would be no Y2K problems with tombstones. Thanks for that update, Captain Obvious.

Women in England were told to bring flashlights with them to the hospital in case the power went out during labor and delivery. Apparently, in addition to dentists, they don't have generators in England either.

Porta Potti rentals were way up. Whoever came up with that one was extremely forward-thinking. Either that or they had a bad sense of priorities. If I thought civilization was ending I'd be busy stocking up on guns, ammo, food, and water, myself. In the case of Y2K, I was in a bar in Iowa with friends doing shots of tequila all night. It turned out it was a better use of my time.

A Florida city near Orlando requested an ordinance change so people could keep livestock within the city limits. Ostensibly this was so that people could do some goat or cattle farming inside city limits after Y2K somehow threw us back to living off subsistence agriculture. Having been in the area recently, I can say that it doesn't appear that law was ever changed back.

Many companies kept their employees working through midnight December 31, so many of them decided to throw parties to keep their employees occupied. No word on how well dozens of drunk computer techs would have dealt with any real problems that turned up. Luckily it wasn't an issue.

Twenty-five percent of people in a random media poll said it was important to have a date on New Year's Eve 1999 because "the world might end, making it their last date." Everyone wants to go out with a bang, I suppose.

Finally, on January 1, 2000, the sun rose and the power was still on. And I didn't wake up till past noon, at least. I don't really remember when, too hung over. So it's possible the sun didn't really come up, but I'm fairly certain it did on January 2.

Now let's take a step back. What really could have gone wrong? Experts predicted things like nuclear power plant failure but never really explained how the hell a nuclear power plant would shut off if it thought the year was 1900 rather than 2000. I'm not saying it's impossible, but what happened was that where systems failed to represent the date correctly, people just manually changed the date on paper and worked around it. One of the "disasters" of Y2K was a pharmacy that had to go to paper transactions when its credit card readers shut down. It was fixed within twenty-four hours. Other problems included people born in the first decade of the 1900s getting automated notices to enroll in public school. Oh, the humanity.

Let's assume for a minute that Y2K was a real problem. How did the entire world manage to get its collective crap together and deal with a specific problem effectively enough to prevent ALL major problems from occurring? Not a goddamn thing caused anyone harm or killed anyone. Not directly anyhow. A Milwaukee man incorrectly stored cans of gasoline in his basement, and later his house burned down. Police at the time said they thought the two events might be related.

Based on the world's track record at solving other problems like war, famine, strip clubs, and lack of the Ten Commandments in courthouses, I suggest to you that the Y2K problem was complete and utter horseshit. Let us also consider that third-world countries, which spent little or no time fixing their Y2K problems, had no major incidents to report either. *Wired* magazine also reported on a survey by Weiss Ratings that indicated that 94 of the largest 496 companies surveyed either had not budgeted enough money for or had not spent any money allocated to Y2K issues. People who were involved in the fix will argue all day long that it was not a waste of time. Unfortunately there is ample evidence that it was.

If Y2K wasn't enough for you, "experts" have kindly predicted a number of other dates that would end civilization as we know it. One was 2/29/00. The leap year rule is that February 29 occurs every four years EXCEPT in years ending in 00 EXCEPT when the year is divisible by 400. Fortunately most computer programmers apparently forgot about the 100/400-year rule and thus the systems performed as normal. Good luck in 2100, though, folks.

In the unlikely event that we don't migrate to 64-bit architectures by 2038 (highly unlikely), we'll have a 2038 problem. However, the fix is in the works for this one, setting us up for a potential

Y290B (B for billion) problem. If I remember my high school astrophysics correctly, the sun will have flared out, taking the earth with it, so it shouldn't be a problem. If I'm still around when that happens, no doubt I'll be hung over that day too.

Sadly, we didn't have comments on Fark at the time of Y2K.

APPARENTLY, HIGH SCHOOL KIDS HAVE THIS NEW THING CALLED "FRIENDS WITH BENEFITS."

Being involved in local TV news in the twenty-first century has to suck. Back in the day, people didn't actually get their news in a timely fashion. Local news used to be able to run pieces on national events. Nowadays everyone is on the Internet and watching twenty-four-hour news channels. As a result, local TV has nothing left to talk about other than people who were murdered around town, whether or not it's going to rain, and local high school sports scores. No doubt this is a real challenge for anyone trying to fill twenty-two minutes with interesting programming.

One tactic local TV news uses to fill the time is to have a roving news team checking out tips from their viewing audience. These tips consist mostly of complaints of businesses ripping people off or government not filling in potholes and so on. First, the TV station catches someone on camera, hidden or otherwise, doing something shady. Then later, a cameraman and a local anchor literally ambush the target, either on the street or at their place of business, and blitz them with questions before they realize what's going on. Television media loves this tactic, called Ambush Journalism. It makes for great TV and usually embarrasses the living hell out of whoever they're going after. Not surprisingly, all of reality TV is founded on the same premise.

Local TV especially loves the segments about kids getting in trouble that parents don't know about. This plays into the worst fears of every parent everywhere, that their kids will be maimed or killed by something the parents should have known about already. In this particular article, the subject is Friends with Benefits. I'm not sure where the age cutoff is for people who are either not familiar with the term or never actually participated in it in some form. Maybe there isn't one. For the five people reading this book who don't already know what Friends with Benefits is, it's kids (or adults) having sex with each other while not in romantic relationships. Shock. Horror. Who gives a rat's ass?

Apparently someone on local TV does. Perhaps it's because their core demographic is people with walkers who are convinced that today's youth have gone to hell in a handbasket. Articles like this just confirm their worldviews. You can tell you're getting old when articles like this about kids start to worry you. I call it Get Off My Lawn syndrome. You're old when you're screaming at kids to get off your lawn, having forgotten that you used to get yelled at for the same thing when you were a kid.

The article opens with a definition of Friends with Benefits, followed by the ominous warning: "Local students say it's happening in high schools right here in Tennessee Valley." Let us not forget that local students also like to say things just to piss you off and intentionally give people wrong directions. We're not talking about the most reliable population segment here. That being said, of course it's happening in your local area. It has since time began. And as long as there are horny guys and gals who are emotionally unavailable, it'll keep on happening.

Now the article starts to heap it on: "We talked with teens whose identities won't be revealed. They say the whole idea has grown into a weekend activity for some." That's your cue to be horrified. Then comes this gem:

> "You know, you go out on a date—dinner and a movie some-times," a Huntsville teen said. "You know, just as friends. And then afterwards, there's the benefits. It's like a drug almost. You know where you can get it and you know where you can get it cheap. And that's where you go."

If anything ever screamed media bullshit, this is it. It's just flat-out not news that teens who go on dates sometimes have sex. And no doubt the producer started jumping up and down for joy the minute the kid being interviewed threw the word *drug* in there in a useless context. Then there's the last statement, which basically equates to "guys know which gals are easy, and they try to have sex with them." Sounds pretty normal to me.

Then the article devolves into the potential downsides. They start with the mental problems, the low self-worth and the like. Then they progress into VDs, AIDS, and pregnancy. So if you're into Friends with Benefits, you're going to be a quivering preg-nant wreck who will die an early death from some disease that probably itches your crotch. And you deserve it. Let that be a les-son to you.

» Numb_Elvis
  Yet another thing that has been going on since the beginning of time that is suddenly a problem because mass media reported on it. woo

» Tricycleracer
  "It also opens the door to sexually transmitted diseases, including AIDS, and pregnancy."
    Because sex with someone you care about makes STDs and pregnancy an impossibility.

» Jayhawk88

Yeah, because all the other times when teenagers were having sex with each other for the past 5,000 years, it has always led to monogamous, committed relationships.

» Olbeal

I didn't know pregnancy was an STD.

» Adman12

If all this new-fangled teen sexuality keeps up, they may have to change the name from "Huntsville" to something beginning with a "C."

» Ryosen

"Chuntsville"?

» Pair-o-dice

this is a new concept? I graduated high school back in '86, and I had "friends w/ benefits"

» MarshWoman

Nothing new under the sun . . . this was going on in my high school in the 70's.

» Tbonefence

Wow, its as if the boomers forgot about the 60's and 70's, you know, the "sexual revolution." Haha, oh yeah . . . that . . .

Not saying this didn't exist before the 60's, but come on parental generation, you were the ones who STARTED this whole thing, don't be surprised it didn't stop when you grew up

» Mcsey

They wrote that whole story without a mention of Seinfeld. Unfarking-believable. Surely they are not that clueless.

FWB's never ends badly emotionally. If it does, it wasn't FWB. It was "a romantic relationship" or "significant other" or however you care to phrase it.

» Binnster

Meh. All I ever got at school was "friends with head-of-nits."

NEWSFLASH: EARTH HAS LEFT ITS ORBIT AND IS HURLING TOWARD THE SUN.

Note that the tagline says "hurling," not "hurtling." . . .

On December 17 we received this link submission simultaneously from two local TV stations in west central Missouri. It was probably sent in by the station's weather guys because I can't imagine who the hell else would be sitting over the NOAA teletype (National Oceanic and Atmospheric Administration—the government weather folks) waiting for notices to come in. Given that both links came in at the same time from two different places, I suspect that once they saw the news bulletin, they just had to send it in to Fark.

My guess is that someone over at the NOAA was testing something by typing in a fake test message, because otherwise it makes no damn sense at all. The news item was quickly deleted from the Internet, so here it is in its entirety:

NON PRECIPITATION STATEMENT
URGENT—WEATHER MESSAGE
NATIONAL WEATHER SERVICE KANSAS CITY—PLEASANT HILL MO
1055 AM CST WED DEC 17 2003

. . . TEST . . . TEST . . . TEST . . .

UNUSUALLY HOT WEATHER HAS ENTERED THE REGION FOR
DECEMBER . . . AS THE EARTH HAS LEFT ITS ORBIT AND IS HURLING
TOWARD THE SUN.

MOZ012-021-172251-
ANDREW MO—CLINTON MO—
1055 AM CST WED DEC 17 2003

...EXCESSIVE HEAT WATCH IN EFFECT FROM THIS AFTERNOON TO
LATE TONIGHT...

UNUSUALLY HOT WEATHER WILL OCCUR FOR AT LEAST THE NEXT
SEVERAL DAYS AS THE EARTH DRAWS EVER NEARER TO THE SUN.
THEREFORE...AN EXCESSIVE HEAT WATCH HAS BEEN POSTED.

STAY TUNED TO NOAA WEATHER RADIO AND OTHER LOCAL MEDIA
FOR FURTHER DETAILS OR UPDATES.

$$

HEINLEIN

Even though it was probably a test, it was still an actual offi-
cial NOAA Weather Service Alert. So we ran it as a NewsFlash
on Fark's main page. Hilarity ensued.

» Red_five_s_b

Nice, it was like -10 outside last night.

» Wycco

I thought hurling was part of the winter Olympics?

» Valorumguygee

That's curling.
    Yay! We're flying into the sun! Everybody sin as fast as you can!

» Dinosaur1972

Wait a second, HURLING toward the sun? So the Earth is blowing chunks?

» Rayden166

They can't even tell me what the weather's gonna be accurately tomorrow.
Pfft.

» Dave_Demonic

Well, that's it then, I am pigging out this Christmas.

» **TheDirtyNacho**

Ah dammit I just washed the car.

» **Techmaniac**

I just hurled at the sun too. Tequila will do that to you.

» **TV_Director**

Meteorologists have no sense of humor, I assure you. It will be the same for the next seven days.

» **Jrdncastillo**

We figured this out in physics class once, we have 13 days to live.

» **That's_a_lot_of_nuts**

Do you think there is any significance to the forecaster's name, HEINLEIN, as in Robert A.

Maybe the guy just wanted to fark with us.

NY TIMES: NOAA says world hurtling toward sun. Markets due to close early.

USA TODAY: NOAA issues severe heat warning. Infographic and opinions inside on A3.

WASHINGTON POST: NOAA says world will burn as it hurtles toward the sun. Women and minorites most affected.

Later on, the text on the link changed to the following:

965
WWUS73 KEAX 171825
NPWEAX

URGENT—WEATHER MESSAGE
NATIONAL WEATHER SERVICE KANSAS CITY—PLEASANT HILL MO
1225 PM CST WED DEC 17 2003

MOZ012-021-171930-
ANDREW MO—CLINTON MO—
1225 PM CST WED DEC 17 2003

... THE TEST EXCESSIVE HEAT WATCH IS CANCELLED ...

PLEASE DISREGARD THE PREVIOUS NPWEAX MESSAGE. IT WAS A
TEST MESSAGE.

$$

NOONAN

Is Media Fearmongering warranted or not? Tomorrow we could
have a massive earthquake along the New Madrid Fault, for ex-
ample. Then I'll appear like an idiot for saying it was stupid to
worry about it.

Take 9/11. After the shock wore off, Congress, the media, and
pretty much every other interest group out there demanded to
know how the U.S. government had let it happen. Today no one
remembers that on 9/10/2001 no one gave a crap about terrorism.
We all thought it couldn't happen in the United States. We'll be
right back to that attitude in a short while if no more attacks oc-
cur, assuming we're not there already.

I can sum up the main weakness of Media Fearmongering
with a sentiment expressed by a friend of mine when we were
kids. He had to go to traffic school because of too many points off
his license (although really, why else would you go?). Back then,
the Kentucky Transportation Cabinet or whoever the hell was in
charge of traffic school used to show pictures of horrible car ac-
cidents as part of the class. They don't do that anymore; someone
probably sued them.

I remember sitting around one night talking to my friend
about it. He summed the experience up like this: "Those photos
scared me so bad I wore my seat belt for a whole two weeks!"
That pretty much sums up the general public's reaction to Me-
dia Fearmongering. Even when it's legitimate, we don't care.

Even when it happens, we soon forget. The general public only gets motivated to action once something has actually happened.

If bird flu had killed 1.7 million people last year, everyone would panic. We'd have 72-point-font headlines screaming about the end of the world, riots in the streets, and general societal collapse if Mass Media is to be believed, given its dire bird flu predictions. It turns out that 1.7 million happens to be the number of people killed by tuberculosis in 2004. Three million people would be even worse, right? That's how many people died from AIDS worldwide in 2004. Nobody is panicking.

For that matter, when was the last time you saw an exposé on The Dangers of Driving? And I don't mean teenagers or old people driving; they do those stories fairly often. I mean young and middle-aged adults driving. Mass Media will get completely bent over massively unlikely events like shark attacks and meteors colliding with the earth, but rarely do you ever hear anything about driving. Look at it this way: Do you know anyone who's ever been bitten by a shark? No. Do you know anyone who's been hurt while on a commercial aircraft? Most likely you don't. Do you know anyone who's ever been hurt while in a car? We all know several people who have been hurt in a car. Odds are most of you know at least one person who died in one. Worse yet, odds are extremely high that you currently know someone who eventually will die in a car crash. It could even be you. Where's the media coverage on this outrageously dangerous thing we call driving? There rarely is any coverage given to this because no one cares. We've grown used to the idea that we'll probably get into a car wreck at some point, and probably sooner rather than later. We've become so used to the idea that we ignore it completely. Hence, no public interest, and thus no media coverage.

As a result, Media Fearmongering stories tend to always cover somewhat unlikely events. Recently I read of an initiative to require car manufacturers to install sensors that alert drivers when they leave a baby in the backseat accidentally. Along those same lines, there is an off switch for the passenger-side airbag in my car, a device that managed to cause only 30–40 deaths ever. By comparison, more people die every year from drinking too much water. Should Congress legislate safety shutoff valves for faucets? Should they ration our water to keep us from drinking too much?

Mass Media can't win on this one. They can't report on the truly dangerous issues of our day, because it doesn't make for a compelling story. No one gets excited enough to care. We all know driving a car is dangerous; we accept it as part of life. Should we? That's debatable.

Unpaid Placement Masquerading as Actual Article

YOU MAY HAVE NOTICED A RECURRING THEME OF THIS BOOK IS that one of the determining factors of journalistic worthiness is laziness. Nothing embodies laziness quite like the Unpaid Placement Masquerading as Actual Article.

Several wire services exist for the sole purpose of collecting press releases from various interest groups, political activist organizations, and the fairly occasionally all-out whack-job cult. These services collate press releases to make it easier for the media to digest them and, with any luck, hopefully pick up and report an item as news. To that end, oftentimes not only are the press releases picked up as articles, they're usually picked up word for word with no changes whatsoever.

Some press releases are newsworthy. For example, you'd want to know about a particular brand of laptop that might burst into flames while you are working on it. Politicians often make or respond to allegations via press releases. Other examples include hurricane warnings, new scientific discoveries, declarations of intent to run for public office, and Amber Alerts. All of these things are news items that most people would like to know about, in some cases as soon as possible.

Other press releases are completely worthless. Many are just alternate forms of advertising, seeking to get press coverage for a particular product or service. Some are opinions masquerading as scientific polls or research studies. Groups representing a particular viewpoint will build "scientific" analysis around it and issue press releases written to make it appear as if their issue is proven to be valid.

Taco Bell is a great example of a company that uses Unpaid Placement Masquerading as Actual Article to great effect. Past stunts of theirs have generated quite a bit of media attention. For example, a few years back they deployed a huge floating target in the Pacific Ocean. They then announced they would give everyone in North America two free tacos if the Mir Space Station crashed into it on reentry into Earth's atmosphere. Another classic promotion gave away gasoline with each meal (come to Taco Bell, get gas).

Taco Bell's sister company, Long John Silver's (also owned by Yum! Brands), tried their hand at media event advertising, but ran into a snag. Long John's announced that if NASA's Mars Exploration Rovers found evidence of large bodies of water on Mars, they would give everyone in North America two free shrimp. They received decent media coverage just for making the offer. Unluckily for Lohn John Silver's, the Rovers did indeed find evidence of oceans on Mars. The restaurant chain initially tried to back out of the deal but soon changed their minds. They must have realized that not many people would show up at their restaurants and order only two shrimp (although no doubt several cheap bastards did).

A few types of Press Releases Masquerading as Actual Article regularly make mainstream news, and by regularly I mean just about every single day. By far the most common of these is the (choose one of each of the following) Top/Bottom 10/25/50/100

Whatevers of the Decade/Century/All Time list. After reading practically every news story that saw print since 1999, I found this type of Unpaid Placement Masquerading as Actual Article annoys me the most. Mainly because there is no creativity involved. That, and I see them on an almost daily basis. The concept is simple: Concoct an arbitrary Top Whatever list (Top Movies of All Time), put at least one controversial choice in the top five (*Bill & Ted's Excellent Adventure*), and omit at least one obvious contender completely (*Citizen Kane*). I've even seen one Top 10 Most Influential Movies list that included *Debbie Does Dallas* at number seven. They absolutely put that in there to get people talking about their list, and it worked too. Getting these Top 10 lists printed is as easy as faxing a press release to Mass Media outlets. Sometimes Mass Media will even hold the articles until news gets slow.

If you come up with a Top 10 list, you can also rewrite it and rerelease it the same day every year so that it becomes the Annual Top Whatever List of All Time. For example, *FHM* and *Maxim* magazines both roll out a hottest babes of the year list around Memorial Day every year, and both get decent media exposure out of it. Everyone's mad that so-and-so didn't make the list, and everyone's shocked that what'shername is in the Top 10. No one ever questions whether these lists are pretty much arbitrary (they are). *FHM* in recent years has added online voting to increase the "legitimacy" of the poll. Now readers can get angry at the unseen masses for leaving their favorite hot chick out of the Top 10 again this year, and morning radio DJs can debate which of the chicks in the polls have the nicer racks. They're great time wasters.

It seems like the Web site AskMen.com managed to generate nearly all of its audience by releasing a steady stream of Top 10 lists to get publicity, such as the Top 10 Sandwiches of All Time,

Top 10 Hot Cars of the Eighties, etc., and so on. It was a successful strategy. News Corporation eventually slurped them up for a bazillion dollars. No word on what they'll use this treasure trove of bullshit Top 10 lists for; they'll probably just end up running them on the Fox News crawl from now until eternity.

The other most common type of Unpaid Placement Masquerading as Actual Article is the Bullshit Scientific Study. These are dressed up to appear as actual legitimate studies but in reality are either heavily manipulated statistics from unscientific polls at best, or at worst, complete and utter made-up crap. Most often, the organization sponsoring the poll or study has a vested interest in the result. At the very least they have an interest in being associated with the particular subject at hand. *FHM* and *Maxim's* Top Hot Chick polls fit into this category as well. Consider the message: *FHM* and *Maxim* are the true guardians of the definitive hot chick polls. All other polls are garbage; only *FHM* and *Maxim* can designate a true winner.

This is also known as branding, which is roughly defined as making your company or product's name synonymous with a particular market sector. I say soft drink, you think Coke or Pepsi. I say phone company, you think AT&T. I say conservatively biased media, you think Fox News. I say broken-ass junky cars, you think any major U.S. automaker. That's an example of branding gone wrong, by the way. Contrary to popular opinion, all publicity is not good publicity.

Incidentally, we at Fark.com have given Unpaid Placement advertising a shot. Fleet Bank announced soon after its merger with Citicorp that it did not intend to continue paying for the naming rights for the Fleet Center in Boston. They decided to auction off naming rights for the Fleet Center for several days on eBay and donate the money to charity. Not surprisingly the online casino Golden Palace bought the first one.

Fark.com bid on one and managed to land a Monday when there were no scheduled events for just over $3,000 (it was all for charity). Initially, we tried to name it the Fark.com Duke Sucks Center, but management over at the center wouldn't go for it. It turns out that one of the three Celtics coaches at the time had a son who played for Duke, though it's unlikely they would have gone for it anyhow. (A Farker did suggest testing them by trying to call it Fark.com Yankees Suck Center, which I think probably would have been accepted.) After putting the question to our readers, and running through such classic suggestions as the Fark .com UFIA Center and the Fark.com Abe Vigoda Memorial Center (Abe wasn't dead at the time), we finally settled on just the plain old Boston Garden.

The backstory here is that Boston Garden was the name of the structure that had been torn down and replaced by the Fleet Center. When it was announced that the new building was going to be named the Fleet Center, there was huge public outcry from the people of Boston. Most were against selling the naming rights to the center, but the Fleet Center prevailed as the name. When we were deciding on a name, I received dozens of e-mail requests literally begging me to name it the Boston Garden. So we did it. This got us another round of media attention. Incidentally, the company that finally bought the naming rights renamed it the TD Banknorth Garden. I suspect that they had seen the publicity Fark got for naming it the Boston Garden. Their name is about halfway there, at any rate. We'll take credit for that. Can't prove it, though.

An interesting corollary to this media pattern that has popped up in recent years is advertisers getting a TV commercial banned on purpose. This seems counterintuitive, but it works amazingly well. A company intentionally concocts an offensive commercial and has it produced professionally. It then submits it to a TV network to be added into rotation with the other ads. The network rejects it. Subsequently, the company in question raises a big stink about it in the media and puts the original commercial on its Web site for download. The result is a huge surge in traffic to the company's Web site from curious people looking to download the banned commercial in question. I highly suspect Ford did this during Super Bowl XXXIX, when it submitted a commercial to Fox that depicted a Catholic priest lovingly (and somewhat sexually) caressing a Ford F-150. The commercial was rejected, Ford complained in the media, and millions of people went to Ford.com to voluntarily download a commercial for Ford trucks.

HOLY HOLE IN A DONUT, BATMAN! ED MCMAHON BEATS ROBIN AS GREATEST SIDEKICK EVER.

Here is a classic example of the Top 10 list. Although in this case it's a Top 50 list, the same principle applies.

Entertainment Weekly at one point produced a Top 50 Sidekicks of All Time list. Everyone from the AP to Reuters to CNN to Fox News to damn near every radio station in the country covered this story. Although it's not really a story, it's a list. The only thing that actually happened here is that *Entertainment Weekly* released a list.

According to the list, Ed McMahon is the greatest sidekick ever, a guy who anyone aged twenty or younger has never even seen on TV other than when he shills for Publishers Clearing House. Yes, it's been that long since Johnny Carson went off the air. I was in middle school at the time; I barely remember it myself.

Number two was Robin of Batman and Robin fame, followed by George Costanza, Chewbacca, and Ethel Mertz. Who is Ethel Mertz? Exactly my point.

The article continues by naming a few other notable people on the list. Then it ends. The total writing time consumed by this piece of garbage can likely be measured in cigarettes smoked while typing it. I'm putting my money on "one." Essentially, the author of the article is reporting on a Top 50 list printed by *Entertainment Weekly*. Talk about a nonevent.

Implicit in the designation Top Whatever list is that the list was reached empirically. Take *U.S. News & World Report*'s annual Best Colleges list, for example. They list multiple criteria used in selecting their top colleges and universities. Some (myself included) would still argue that it's bullshit to rank one college as fifteenth best and one as sixteenth best. But whatever, they've invented a model to rank colleges with, and they put a lot of work into it. Good for them. I could give a rat's ass, but some people like it.

Compare this with what *Entertainment Weekly* did. The article actually states that *EW*'s staff chose the list. Not that you could empirically choose a list of top sidekicks based on certain qualities, but most media consumers don't stop to consider whether it's even possible in the first place. Media consumers assume that if there's a Top Whatever list, especially when the list was generated by a recognizable media name, someone in charge must have had great rationale and impeccable scientific methods to reach the results. Which is obviously not what happened with *EW*'s Top Sidekicks list. What we have instead is a list, compiled by a bunch of staffers, of arbitrarily ranked sidekicks designed with the sole purpose in mind of pissing you off when you read it so you go complain to someone and give their sucky list more media coverage. Maybe you'll even go buy a copy of *EW*. That's what they're hoping you'll do, anyhow. *EW* managed to spread this out over a whopping eighteen pages on their Web site, meaning anyone who went to visit probably clicked on them all, and generated a ton of ad impressions in the process.

Aside from the issue that this Top 50 list is bogus, the greater question is why do CNN, AP, Reuters, and other sources think this Top 50 list warrants any kind of media coverage? Because it will fill space on a slow news day, and no one will question its presence in that day's batch of articles. These lists exist solely as commercials for the folks who originate them. And that includes *U.S. News & World Report*'s Best Colleges list. It's probably a decent guide for colleges, but the main reason they print it is because, these days, it's the only thing this magazine does that you have actually heard of. Other than lose money hand over fist as they sink into obscurity.

Note how the Farker comments consist solely of arguments about who should and should not be on the list.

» Jay Gielle_Unemployed Hawaiian Ninja_Ph.D
And tonto's not even on the list. how shameful.

» Cloptimus
What about Twiggy from Buck Rodgers or Boxy from BattleStar Galactica? They are biased against robots.

» Buttertownmayor
I would just like to point out that the list features Art Garfunkel as Paul Simon's sidekick.

» Worst.Poster.Ever.
More of the man puttin' the wookie down. Han Solo was Chewbacca's sidekick, not the other way around, muthafarkers.

[ABOUT FLORIDA] WHERE ELSE CAN A 20-OUNCE HAMBURGER MADE WITH MEAT FROM THREE CONTINENTS COST $100?

Actually, the answer to the question is: pretty much anywhere.

Another common form of Unpaid Placement Masquerading as Actual Article is Oh My God They're Charging How Much for What? You probably can't think of any specific examples off the top of your head but no doubt you remember seeing them before: $1,000 for a mint julep at the Kentucky Derby; $5,000 a night for a hotel room in NYC; $500 for the world's largest ice-cream sundae. And here we have the $100 hamburger.

Mass Media is being blatantly manipulated to give free press, and to top it all off they're complicit. Here's the general thought process: Restaurant needs publicity. Restaurant creates menu item so expensive no one will ever order it. Write press release about how freaking expensive said menu item is, then (and this is the important part) also announce that you will donate some or all of the money raised to charity. This will guarantee that some idiot trying to cash in on some free publicity will buy it for the tax write-off, generating another round of free media coverage for all involved.

It's also annoying that in this particular case, super-expensive hamburgers have been done before. Many times. DB Bistro Moderne in New York City is listed in the Guinness World Records as having the most expensive hamburger, at $120, a dubious title at best since as of right now I would like to declare that I'm selling hamburgers out of my very own fridge for $150. Any takers?

Seriously, is that all we need to do to get news coverage? Aggressive pricing?

From the article: "The meat is also available via mail. [Marc] Sherry said orders for the burly burgers have already been placed by 1960s crooner Paul Anka and former Van Halen frontman David Lee Roth." Note that the Press Release/Article mentions two guys badly in need of free publicity. For example, who knew Paul Anka was still alive? It's probably not worth noting that one misplaced comma and you'd be led to believe Paul Anka was the lead singer of Van Halen.

Not only have these types of articles been done before, but worse, even the guy who runs the restaurant in the article has done this before. In 2002, Marc Sherry launched a $41 Kobe beef burger at his New York restaurant. He later went back to the well a second time by selling a $19 hot dog at his restaurant in Atlantic City. Apparently he needed some extra publicity for his Boca Raton restaurant in 2006. So why not do the same thing? The media just runs this crap for free, no point in advertising anywhere.

» Nelsonal

At most every airport cafe in the country. Pilots joke about the hundred dollar hamburger which means you fly half an hour eat lunch and fly home. It costs about $100 per hour of operating light aircraft.

» Griz212

"We let the meat do all the talking," said assistant chef Joseph Galison.
. . . uhhh . . . in that case . . . make mine well done.

» Hilary T. N. Seuss

It's almost as if they're trying to sell the idea that imitating David Lee Roth is some sign of prestige. How odd.
As for Paul Anka—"Just don't look! Just don't look!"

» Absinthe

And you know that at least 1/3 of the people who order this ask for well done.

» Char_boy

What? No interview with Jimmy Buffett about this one? Florida, what's wrong with you?

"ALIEN HEAD" X-RAY GETS $9,600 IN AUCTION—COURTESY OF THE SAME CASINO THAT BOUGHT WILLIAM SHATNER'S KIDNEY STONE.

The International Bird Rescue Research Center of Cordelia, California, posted an X-ray of a duck online. I'm not really sure how anyone came across it, but it became a brief Internet phenomenon as people forwarded copies of the duck's X-ray via e-mail. The interest stemmed from the fact that the X-ray appeared to depict an object inside the duck that looked like the head of an alien of *Close Encounters* or *X-Files* fame.

Now let's not kid ourselves here, there's no way in hell there's an alien head in a duck, real or otherwise. This article almost qualified as an example of Equal Time for Nutjobs, but didn't quite make the cut because the media made only the slightest of passing mentions that maybe there really was an alien head inside a sick duck. Surprisingly, no one interviewed any alien head "experts." I'm not even sure there is such a thing, which may explain why that didn't happen.

The center had the bright idea to put the X-ray up on eBay. As I've mentioned before, the media loves to be able to run stories more than once. The fact that anyone would buy an X-ray of an alien head in a duck is easily worth devoting an entire article to it, in the minds of news editors everywhere. Never mind that someone will buy the item for an absurd amount of money every single time like clockwork because (1) the proceeds go to charity because they're tax-deductible and (2) everyone likes the free media coverage.

Enter the Golden Palace Casino.

The undisputed master of getting media attention is Golden Palace Casino, an online gambling Web site. They got their start in media manipulation by getting boxers to wear temporary tattoos of ads during fights, a move which always prompted media discussion of the tattoos during the matches. Later this evolved into putting tattoos on streakers at sporting events, which worked for obvious reasons. Personally I think they probably had more success when they were sponsoring male streakers, because the one time I saw them sponsor a female streaker (who was a porn star at that), I didn't realize until later, once I had read a news article, that it was one of their stunts. The streaker was just too smoking hot; it didn't even register with me that she had tattoos. Note, though, that the ploy did work. They succeeded in getting free media coverage.

Sometime in late 2004 Golden Palace hit on the idea of buying at weird eBay auctions. By weird I mean truly weird, like a grilled cheese sandwich with the Virgin Mary's face on it, the PopeMobile, and various permanent tattoos on people and small children. If you look up their profile on eBay you can see the entire litany. Not surprisingly, their feedback is excellent; yours would be too if you paid thousands of dollars over cost to spray-paint a herd of cows with your corporate logo. WOULD SELL TO AGAIN A++++++++++++. Most recently, they issued a press release saying they were considering opening up a museum with all their odd purchases on display.

Lately, Golden Palace has been on a slight hiatus from buying weird crap on eBay. The main problem is Media Fatigue; not only was everyone tired of reading about Golden Palace buying things like rags used to wipe down beached whales or William Shatner's kidney stones, but even worse, the media was starting to leave out mention of their full name. Instead of Golden Palace, the media would say the items were purchased by "an online casino" that would remain unnamed in the article, completely defeating the purpose of buying the eBay items in the first place.

It so happens that time is shorter on the Internet than in real life. As a result it's possible to go from worn out to retro hip in the same calendar year. Thus, when Golden Palace found itself unable to resist purchasing the Alien Head Duck X-Ray, massive media coverage ensued on all the major news outlets. I'm not exaggerating: all of them. Golden Palace paid a tax-deductible $9,600 for the X-ray and got better media coverage than if they had actually paid for commercials. Which, incidentally, they can't legally do thanks to their being an online casino.

» Prime-8

So WTF was the thing inside the duck?

» Spork Bunny

The leading hypothesis is that it was actually a small weather balloon, filled with swamp gas. Or the duck had a bad case of swamp gas.

Ducks spend a lot of their time in swamps you know.

» AlrightGuy

Am I the only one who originally misread "sick duck" in the opening paragraph?

Come on in, the gutter's fine.

PROVING THAT MORE PEOPLE ENJOY LYING TO POLLSTERS THAN WATCHING FOOTBALL, "VEGETABLES" TOPS SURVEY OF MOST POPULAR SUPER BOWL SNACKS.

Opinion polls share a common flaw with lie detectors: They only measure what a person believes he does as opposed to what a person actually does. This is evident in the disparity between actual obesity rates in the United States and percentages reported by polls asking the question "Are you a giant fatass?" People don't think they are fat. They also believe some other bizarre things about themselves. One of those things, certainly far off the radar in the general scheme of things, is a recent survey by the NPD Group, a market researcher for industries of every ilk. The survey indicated that the most popular snacks for the Super Bowl are vegetables.

This is complete horseshit. The only things people use vegetables for during the Super Bowl is as a garnish. Vegetables are like the exercise bike in your basement; you have them around only so you'd have the option to use them, but you never really get around to it.

The article opens up with the following bold statement:

> What appears to be a first leading up to Super Bowl XL is that the most popular snacks millions will munch in front of television are now vegetables.

So if I'm the above-average reader and I get that far into the article, I automatically reach the conclusion that people must be eating nothing but vegetables now. Man, am I an idiot. I'm so behind

the times. I should be serving nothing but vegetables at my Super
Bowl party just like everyone else does.

But pay close attention to what else the poll actually says:

> Vegetables were eaten at nearly 30 percent of all dinners on
> Super Bowl Sunday for the last five years, beating out potatoes,
> sandwiches, salads, salty snacks, and even the venerable pizza
> and chicken wings.

Wait a second. In the first paragraph they said it was a "first"
that vegetables are the most popular snacks, now they're telling us
this has been going on for five years? That would make this the
fifth time then, by my count, not the first.

And if vegetables were eaten at 30 percent of all dinners on
Super Bowl Sunday, it would appear that 70 percent of Americans
said they didn't eat vegetables at all for dinner. It's also interesting
that salads and potatoes don't count as vegetables. I'm not sure
how they decided that was the case. I don't believe I've ever had
a meat salad before. The article also doesn't say whether salsa and
guacamole count as vegetables, in which case maybe the poll re-
searchers are on to something after all. Come to think of it, tech-
nically speaking, potato chips and corn chips are vegetable-based
as well.

Now comes the first warning flag that indicates this "study" is
complete and utter crap:

> NPD Vice President Harry Balzer said he knows traditionalists
> will challenge the findings....

Nothing screams bogus science like an opening salvo at the
unbelievers who refuse to see what is obviously such a compelling
argument. The article says that if you disagree with these findings,

you're a "traditionalist." It's not enough to just present data; the article has to attack those who might doubt its findings. No word on why left-leaning politicos who complain that the word "liberal" has been hijacked by the right and changed into an insult don't start yelling "traditionalist" back at them. By attacking people who might contradict the study, the press release has already begun to try to deflect analysis of their claim. Anyone with a different opinion will first have to answer to the accusation that he is a "traditionalist."

Additionally, could Harry Balzer even be a real name? What are the odds anyone could survive their teenage years with a name like Harry Balzer? Slim to none, I'd say.

That's pretty much the entire article, which appeared in all the major newswires. Here's the problem: Assuming this article wasn't completely made up, it was based on a poll of people's opinions of what they really ate. The media in this case doesn't question their methods. Did the journalist immediately start making calls to find out if the poll was done accurately? Did they look into the polling methods used? Did they check to see what kind of bias the NPD had? Nope. It's a copy-and-paste job, no questions asked.

By the way, one of NPD's clients, is, you guessed it, the Produce Marketing Association. You just read an unpaid commercial masquerading as news.

» markie_farkie

Like I'd trust a survey published by someone named Harry Balzer.

» Beavosaurus Rex

I'm thinking that BEER is the most popular snack. Vegetables? Puhhhhhlease . . .

» Redford Renegade

I'm making some vegetables* for my guests.

*All vegetables will be wrapped in bacon or deep-fried.

» DigitalStrange

So an entire category of food beats out any one other type of food item?
Wow, whooda thunk?

  If I have 10 pizzas and 1 bowl of celery sticks at my party and my next
door neighbor has 1000 wings and one plate of carrot sticks then the
veggies win the way they did the survey.

» Mastethom

Lying to pollsters is why I've regularly gotten invitations to join the AARP in
the mail since I was 25.

» HairBonus

The obvious correlation: only 30% of Super Bowl parties will have women
at them.

MORE THAN 60 PERCENT OF BRITONS USE SCREWDRIVERS, SCISSORS, KNIVES, KEYS, AND EARRINGS TO FLOSS.

This article is the classic form of Unpaid Placement Masquerading
as Actual Article. So you form a dental foundation in Great Britain. That's all well and good, but how do you get publicity for your
foundation? By making up a BS press release of course. You even
give it an official-sounding name, in this case the National Dental
Survey, which makes it sound like the government had something
to do with it. Then send it to the media. They'll summarize the
"findings," and it'll see print.

  In this particular case, the Dental Health Foundation created
a phone survey where 60 percent of the respondents reported that

they pick their teeth with screwdrivers, earrings, and scissors. Or anything else that happens to be lying around. To me the larger point in the same article was that the study found that 23 percent of Britons didn't pick their teeth at all.

But this all assumes that the study was actually valid. Let's examine what is lacking in this article. Who the hell are these Dental Health Foundation people? You and I can go out tomorrow and found the National Plumbers Foundation without being plumbers or having any particular experience in the field. Was their poll statistically random or did they just go around the office and ask people to make up bogus answers? How many people were interviewed? What questions did they ask? Do the 60 percent who pick their teeth with household objects do so regularly or once a decade? The media doesn't care. They don't check on these facts because they're not there, period. The point is, the journalist in question leaped on this opportunity to crank out an article with little or no work, not even bothering to check if this shit is just completely made up.

» Malcy

I use an axe.

» Eddyatwork

I use my elbow.

» Binnster

I use bricks. You don't have any more dental worries (or teeth) if you floss with bricks.

» Gwowen

Hey! Look! We're getting lectured on appearance by the fattest nation the world has ever seen.

Break out the "Big Book Of American Superficiality and Hypocrisy"

» Mungo

I call bullshit. I have never seen or heard of anyone doing anything like this ever.

I can only guess that the question was something like "Have you ever used an odd item to pick your teeth?" If so I can image using a key or something to get an annoying bit of apple skin out if you were having a picnic in the middle of nowhere—but it's hardly a trend, is it?

Utter balls.

» Devil's Advocaat

Don'tcha just love news stories that quote statistical research.

How quickly

"60% of people use items close to hand in order to floss after a meal"

becomes

"60% of people use screwdrivers to brush their teeth."

NOT TO BE OUTDONE BY NEW OXFORD AMERICAN DICTIONARY, WEBSTER'S NAMES "INFOSNACKING" THEIR 2005 WORD OF THE YEAR, EVEN THOUGH NO ONE'S EVER HEARD OF IT OR USED IT IN CONVERSATION.

It really must suck to be a dictionary company these days. Your target demographic, kids required to buy your product for school, is dwindling down to nothing, thanks to the Internet and the fact that Google.com will correct your spelling for you. I'm amazed these guys are still in business.

Given this dire situation, dictionaries have had to become creative to attract attention. What could be more boring than a dictionary? Other than a thesaurus, which we don't need either, thanks to Bill Gates and Microsoft Word.

Every year, the two titans of the dictionary industry go head-to-head in a battle to get the best blatant publicity. And every year the media just prints their press releases without considering what they're actually claiming.

The *New Oxford American Dictionary* started this round of the word wars by releasing another press release that made it into Mass Media. It claimed that the word "podcasting" was the Word of the Year. It didn't make any comment as to the selection criteria. I personally believe it somehow involved a monkey and a dart board. What the hell does it mean to be named Word of the Year anyhow?

Webster's New World College Dictionary wasn't about to let *New Oxford American Dictionary* just get away with all this free press, so they soon followed with their own article. They claimed that "info-snacking" was their Word of the Year. This despite the fact that no one has ever heard anyone say it. They just made it up on the spot.

> "It hasn't caught on yet," admitted Mike Agnes, editor in chief of *Webster's*. But the word of the year isn't about popularity, he explains; there aren't even any plans to add it to the dictionary.
>
> "We try to choose a word that tickles our linguistic funny bone or is significant in the way language reflects culture," Agnes said.

Or, to paraphrase, they actually admitted that they just made this shit up.

» Nytmare

The word of the year is "legs." Spread the word.

» Cyberlost

Oh, I use it all the time.

Kids! Moms brought home da Doritos! We be in'fo'snacking!

» Overlord

They made up a sniglet and then voted it word of the year?

» Mugato

I made up one:

douchebag(n): A person who thinks they're terribly clever by making up a word to describe mindless minutia. They travel in herds and are also seen playing yuppie boardgames, talking about American Idol at the watercooler and quoting "Friends" to each other as if it were isoteric code. Kill on sight.

» Inflatable Jesus

in·fo·snack (v): to invent an imaginary word for a phony press release created solely to promote your new dictionary.

» Whidbey

Personally I would beat anyone to death who used the word freely . . .

» SavageWombat

When you do too much infosnacking, do you have to take an infodump?

THE AWARD FOR "AMERICA'S DUMBEST DRIVERS" GOES TO . . . RHODE ISLAND.

With a lead like that, you might guess this wasn't a very scientific study. You might be wrong. The reason is because the organization in charge of this poll was GMAC Insurance. Insurance companies have their shit together in a serious way. Their entire financial well-being is predicated on their being able to accurately predict what combination of factors indicate that you can't drive worth a crap. As a male who was once single and under twenty-five, I can tell you from experience that the auto insurance industry thinks that particular demographic is most likely to wreck a car, right behind Floridians. The only way it could be worse for you if you are male, under twenty-five, and single is if you live in a state like Pennsylvania, where the deer population is so out of control that your car will be in the shop once a month to fix deer-related car damage.

GMAC's test checked individual drivers' knowledge of the rules of the road. The article goes into quite a bit of boring statistical detail on the methods used in the test. You'd fall dead asleep reading it. Given that, though, I have a suspicion that it was probably all aboveboard and legitimate. The results were that Rhode Island has the dumbest drivers. To me, this was an unusual result because having grown up in and being a current resident of the state of Kentucky, I've come to expect that any study involving a state-by-state ranking on how stupid or fat Americans are will have southern states all clustered at the bottom. But not this time. Suck it, Rhode Island. It turns out Oregon has the smartest drivers.

The study also revealed details such as the fact that one in five respondents weren't aware that pedestrians have the right-of-way. That statement is in the article for shock value, but look at it another way: Only 20 percent of respondents didn't know. Given that 90 percent of any random group of people will be made up of complete dumbasses, a 20 percent failure rate is somewhat reassuring if you think about it.

However legitimate this study may have been, it does not change the fact that this is an Unpaid Placement Masquerading as Actual Article. GMAC and other insurance companies run these kinds of studies all the time to tweak their risk factors so they don't go ass-broke trying to cover everyone's car insurance. GMAC didn't have to release this study to the media; in fact, most of the studies they run never see the light of day. The sole reason this ended up in the media at all was because GMAC wanted publicity. They wrote up a study, issued a press release to the media, and stepped back to see what happened. It worked. All the newswires picked up the story and every morning radio show in the U.S. and Canada talked about their study. But hey, good for them, it's not like they had any control over the media picking up the story. It's not GMAC to blame for exposing the rest of us to this crap, it's Mass Media.

» Drama_Llama

From the article:

46. Maryland
47. New York
48. New Jersey (Tie)
48. Massachusetts (Tie)
50. Washington, D.C.
51. Rhode Island

All blue states, HAH! Suck it, libs!

» HulkHands

Seeing that the test is online, and people in red states are too dump to operate computers, let alone voting devices, I find this poll rather skewed.

» Koch

HulkHands: people in red states are too dump to operate computers.
    Irony, I adore thee.

» Pale_Green_Pants_With_Nobody_Inside_Them

Is RI still a state?

» mr_a

The only reason Oregon could be #1 at something like this is the road signs are so bad that drivers tend to get smarter trying to figure them out.

SOME OF BASEBALL'S WACKIEST PROMOTIONS

This article summed up some of the wackiest minor league base-ball promotions, something near and dear to my heart. In the late nineties my hometown had a minor league hockey team. The Kentucky Thoroughblades were affiliated with the San Jose Sharks. San Jose sucked so badly during those years that they continually raided the minor league team for more players. Things got so bad that ESPN eventually started calling them the San Jose Thoroughblades since at one point half the pro roster had been called up from the minors.

I went to about a dozen or so TBlades games while they were in town. They were actually kind of fun, considering it was (1) minor league and (2) hockey, a sport I don't generally watch. They held dozens of promotions during the game and made sure each stop in play was accompanied by booming bass pop music to either keep the crowd interested in the game or mask the fact that no one was cheering. Or the fact that the crowds were always about 5,000 peo-ple in an arena that seated 23,500.

The TBlades did have some avid fans, however. I could never understand how this could be. The problem as I see it is that the minute you develop an affinity for a particular player, in theory because they're damn good at playing the sport, the parent team calls them up to play at the major league level. I realize this is the whole point to having minor leagues in the first place, but it was a major turnoff for me. I'm pretty sure I'm not the only one who feels this way. This is no doubt why you don't see any 50,000-seat baseball stadiums being built for the Toledo Mud Hens, for example.

Given this inherent problem, minor league teams have to

take other steps to try to bring the crowds into the parks. In recent years, marketing directors have become extremely creative in coming up with promotions that get passed off as mainstream news. They're fairly realistic about it as well. From the article: " 'As much as I like to think people come to us for the baseball, I know better,' said Jack Weatherman, the team's promotions director." Yup, that about sums it up. Weatherman is promotions director for the St. Paul Saints, whose games incidentally sell out on a regular basis in a town that already has a reasonably decent major league baseball team.

According to surveys of the crowds, while very few people say that they come to the games because of the promotions, "41 percent called their biggest reason for coming to games at Midway Stadium: social atmosphere. The baseball action, itself, was the top draw for just 26 percent."

The undisputed master of the newsworthy promotion is Mike Veeck, current owner of the St. Paul Saints. He came by it honestly from his dad, Bill Veeck, who used to do the same sort of things when he owned the Chicago White Sox. Bill's most infamous promotion occurred in 1979, when the team announced that anyone who brought a disco record could trade it in for a 98-cent ticket. During a break mid-game, a Chicago DJ carried a box of records out on the field and blew it up, along with a good part of the field. For some reason this convinced fans that it was a good time to run out onto the field, riot, and set fire to things. Result: 6 injuries, 39 arrests, and the White Sox forfeited the game. Mike later took credit/blame for this promotion as well.

Some of Mike Veeck's previous greatest hits include:

Vasectomy Night: pretty much what you think it was. I don't know if radio stations came up with this first or vice versa; it's still funny, though.

Nobody Night: locking out the fans until the fifth inning so that the official attendance was zero.

Tonya Harding mini-bat night: self-explanatory, really. Veeck managed to get Harding to take time off from her busy schedule to show up and autograph the bats.

Enron Night: Paper shredders were placed at the gates and the announced attendance was later adjusted downward.

Mime-O-Vision Night: Veeck put mimes on top of the dugouts and had them act out plays. This particular promotion ended early because fans began pelting them with hot dogs. Note that no one was throwing beer. Why would you ever throw beer?

The interesting thing about these promotions is that every single press release made national newswires as an article. Most usually made news twice, once when the promotion was announced and once when it actually happened. Occasionally someone would protest one of the stunts, like Vasectomy Night, which was good for another run through the press.

I really enjoyed these stories when they came through on Fark. I can't think of many things funnier than people throwing hot dogs at mimes. While these articles are indeed advertising, they're also pretty entertaining. There's an interesting message here: Sometimes advertising isn't irritating. It's still not news, though.

» zsouthboy

As long as the mime doesn't perform the actual vasectomy.

» Snarfangel

I think there should be a Free Vasectomy Night at professional wrestling events.

» TheShadowsLTH

Mike certainly takes after his father. Bill Veeck was a master showman. Disco demolition night. The shower out in the outfield. Bill would also, according to legend, dress up and go into the stands.

My dad, when he was young, went to White Sox game. After going to a vendor he saw, he later realized, Bill Veeck sitting in a seat. He only realized it later because Veeck was dressed in full Pirate regalia. This was in the late 50s/early 60s so sadly he has no photos of the incident. I'm always amused by it.

» Satchel

Hey, I was at Enron night in Portland. Not only did they mess around with the attendance figures, but all the player stats on the scoreboards were out of whack and they also changed the distances on the outfield fence. Also, if your name was Arthur or Andersen, you got in free.

» GiantTrev

San Jose Giants (A League) Have some of the best promotions:

Beer Batter—A player from the opposing team (usually their best hitter) is chosen as the "beer batter"; if he strikes out, half price beer for 15 minutes. At strike 2, fans are going nuts for a call from blue, and the strike zone widens considerably.

Smash for cash—Three fans each choose a player (non pitcher), and a beat up truck is parked down the first base line. Each player gets two throws to try and smash a headlight. If he does, the fan gets a gift card to a local gas station, or pizza joint or something. If I ever get picked, I'm choosing a catcher.

SEARCH FOR MODERN DESCENDANTS OF GENGHIS KHAN

Fark's tagline:

> Search for modern descendants of Genghis Khan uncovers mild-mannered Miami accounting professor. "I think I do have a certain number of administrative skills. I haven't done any conquering, per se."

Fark's tagline: two weeks later, second article:

> New genetic test determines that Florida professor is not a direct descendant of Genghis Khan, and his propensity to wear furry hats is a mere coincidence.

This is pretty rare; it's a double Unpaid Placement Masquerading as Actual Article. The infosnacking article we discussed earlier is one also. One company will release an Unpaid Placement Masquerading as Actual Article, and another company in the same field will rush to do the same on a similar subject, hoping for similar free publicity.

The first article appears as though it was copied straight from a press release, making it perfect for pickup by Mass Media. I can just see the concept pitch. "See, he's a descendant of Genghis Khan, who was a mean bastard who conquered the entire world, but he's an accountant! Oh my God, what would his great-great-great-great-etc.-etc.-grandfather think of that!" They bought it hook, line, and sinker. I wonder if the guy in question even knew that its mere presence in Mass Media hinged on the fact that Douglas Adams first used this gag in *Hitchhiker's Guide to the Galaxy* and that everyone would automatically assume he was a dork since he was an accounting professor. Probably not.

The article begins: "A British research firm recently combed 25,000 DNA samples searching for a modern descendant of Genghis Khan from outside the Mongolian warlord's ancient empire."

Pretty good so far. We now think this article is about a British research firm (assumption: nonprofit); they have lots of DNA samples from paying customers (assumption: popular, therefore cool); and they're looking for descendants of Genghis Khan (assumption: doing valuable research, as opposed to fooling around, goofing off, or trying to make us believe this isn't a commercial). It isn't until down near the middle of the article that the company's name, Oxford Ancestors, appears in print.

The poor bastard they drag into the media spotlight, Tom Robinson, probably didn't even know what hit him. The point of the article was to establish this guy as a loser; otherwise, who cares that he's related to Genghis Khan? If he were a 300-pound former linebacker and current bounty hunter, the article wouldn't fly for lack of interest, because we'd all expect the great Khan's progeny to be able to kick some serious ass.

The first thing they tell us about him in the article: University of Miami accounting professor with a receding hairline. Nice touch there with the receding hairline. While you're at it, why not tell us he wet the bed till he was eight, never kissed a girl in high school, and was once stuffed in a locker before gym class.

In case we don't yet get the point, they throw this in as well:

They're an unlikely pair, the emperor and the accountant. Genghis was known as the type of guy who would conquer villages across two continents, murder entire tribes and take thousands of female partners. Robinson, on the other hand, just returned from a cruise to Alaska with his wife of 25 years.

Yup, just pour it on. Kick him in the nuts while you're at it.' The Great Khan wouldn't put up with that, but this guy will.

The article goes into light technical details about how the tests work. Then they throw this one out as an afterthought: "No one has tested Genghis' actual DNA because his tomb has never been found." Wait, what? Then how the hell do you know if he's related to Genghis Khan? Answer: They made this crap up.

They toss in a sexual reference too, talking about how Genghis Khan banged every woman in Asia in his time. A little titillation never hurts.

The last half of the article discusses the company, Oxford Ancestors, how much the process costs, what you have to do, where you can get the test, and how so many people have discovered their ancestors were Irish kings and stuff like that. Ooo, now I'm interested. Sign me up.

Bear in mind this was all in an actual news article. This wasn't an infomercial, it was an honest-to-god *Miami Herald* article, later picked up by the Associated Press.

Two weeks later, however, we get some bad news. That poor bastard Tom Robinson is not only *not* related to Genghis Khan, but he's still a loser to boot.

The follow-up article said that Robinson sought out a second opinion from Family Tree DNA to see if he really was related to Genghis Khan. I highly suspect Family Tree DNA contacted him and volunteered a free test on the off chance they could get some free press. Personally, if someone told me I was related to Genghis Khan, I'd just take their word for it. That is unless they pissed me off by making me look like a complete loser in their Unpaid Placement Masquerading as Actual Article. Then I'd want to make them look stupid too.

The second test revealed Robinson and Khan shared a common ancestor but were not directly related. The article then goes on to slam Oxford Ancestors, saying, "But because Genghis Khan's burial place was unknown, the tests are based on probabilities, and Oxford Ancestors' results were initially met with skepticism by some scientists." Those bastards!

> The British company's spokesman, Benjamin Webb, said the firm would be happy to retest Robinson's results according to whatever criteria he set.
>
> "However, it has to be emphasized that according to the criteria employed by Oxford Ancestors Tom Robinson does indeed fulfill the requirements," Webb said. "Before we change our mind and do anything else, we would want to retest."

Well, of course they would. Maybe they'll get another article out of it where Oxford Ancestors can point out that Robinson really is related to Genghis Khan, is still a loser, and Family Tree DNA sucks.

» **Respect the Cock**

1000 years from now, geneticists will probably discover that 1 out of 3 people are also descended from Wilt Chamberlain.

» **Persepolis**

As a Persian, I demand this accountant have to pay reparations to me for Khan destroying Persia.

» **ThrobblefootSpecter**

That's funny. Because my ancestry includes a 13th Century Mongolian accountant.

» **Goobernutz**

He's american? well then he's like

50% Genghis Khan,
25% Cleopatra people,

10% Italian (so he can wear a gold Italian horn),

10% Scotch-Irish (whatever that is. but it gives him an excuse to get extra drunk on St.Patty's day AND wear a kiss me I'm Irish shirt)

3% Apache (they always pick a cool tribe. no one is ever from the Ismakaho tribe) and

2% master barbeque chef.

» RoscoePColtraine

  Miami = Genghis Cohen

» TheForkOfJustice

  Honestly, I'm disgusted in all of you for the lack of Star Trek references.

MAN CREATES BACKYARD ZAMBONI WHICH CAN ALSO SERVE AS A SNOWBLOWER TO CLEAR A DRIVEWAY, MOW A LAWN IN SUMMER, AND SPREAD LIQUID FERTILIZER FROM ITS TANK.

As you can probably guess by the tagline, this article is about a man who made a Zamboni knockoff for use at home in the backyard. Probably not coincidentally, he also invented Porta-Rinx, a portable ice rink for the backyard. The article is kind enough to let us know this as well, just in case we might buy one of those too. Although come to think of it, if you don't already have a backyard ice rink, you probably don't need a backyard Zamboni.

  I included this article here not because it was interesting, although it's not bad, but because it was the purest form of Unpaid Placement Masquerading as Actual Article I have ever seen. It seems the article was "written" and released by the Associated Press, so we have no one to blame for bad writing. However, my hunch is that the only people who had a hand in writing this article were the publicists for the guy who invented all this crap.

We've all read magazines that have paid advertisements in them that look like actual articles. They usually have some indication that they are paid, by saying so at the top of the page and/ or using a different font for the article. This AP article reads exactly like one of those, except it's not a paid article. Someone at the AP decided this press release could stand alone as an actual article. Ridiculous.

Here's the paraphrased article breakdown:

Damian Renzello really wanted a good ice surface for his backyard. This establishes that he's an inventor because he cares, not because he just wants cash in his pocket. By the way, he also invented some other stuff you should check out, like a portable ice rink and a pull-behind Zamboni knockoff. The Bambini Revolution (his name for it) costs about $30,000 in case you want one. Cool.

He has sold 325 ice rinks. He invented the Ice Mower after a client requested a machine to clear the snow off the ice surface. After making it out of a modified riding lawn mower, it could also mow the grass and spread liquid fertilizer. Wow, this thing is great, what can it not do?

And that is the article in its entirety. The only thing being written about is this guy's great product. The entire article is one giant commercial. How the hell this managed to get published as an article escapes me, because when you get right down to it, all this guy did was "invent" the tractor.

» I_Am_Jesus

—NASA should probably hire this guy to fix that foam problem.

» Barking Pumpkin

—I, too, can spread "liquid fertilizer."
Ladies only need apply. No fat chicks.

» Neurocrat

You need to eat more fiber.

» Barking Pumpkin

I see my attempt at wit has been turned to my disadvantage and dismay.
I walk the road of shame.

» DMW Devil

It's good to know that people other than the cell phone/PDA/computer
companies are trying to merge all their products into one. . . .

» Danger Mouse

What's the big deal? I've got a wife who can do all that.

» Bonno

But he didn't get arrested for driving drunk on it along a motorway the wrong
way wearing only a pair of Y-fronts?
I thought this was Fark.

» Pro Zack

So what. My grandfather's tractor could do all that and plow a field.

» Djh0101010

Um, how is this different than my 40 year old John Deere garden tractor with
the snowthrower, mower deck, and a tow-behind sprayer? "invented" is a
pretty strong word for "bolted together a bunch of stuff just like it's been
done for decades."

Since Fark's inception in 1999 we've seen a steady increase in the
number of submissions that are ads masquerading as articles,
funny video clips, blog entries, and the like. The main reason for
this is the nature of today's advertising market. Starting with
Generation X, people began exhibiting somewhat an immunity
to conventional advertising. Starting with Generation Y, people
began spending more time on the Internet than on TV, radio, or

newspapers. The Internet is just about the easiest place to ignore advertising. So what are advertising agencies to do?

Unpaid Placement Masquerading as Actual Article is just another type of product placement. How in the hell are these things seeing print?

The more insidious answer is paid placement, that Mass Media is being paid to run these articles. *Free Press* and the Center for Media and Democracy filed an FCC complaint containing a list of seventy-seven television stations it said had broadcast unattributed video news releases (VNRs, essentially paid placement). These would be news features such as Ask the Local Doctor, where the local doctor in question is paid to give advice during the segment, usually touting his or her products or services along the way. Without the payment, the implication is that the local doctor would never have had a segment on the local news. The FCC investigated and issued formal letters of inquiry to forty-two of those initial seventy-seven stations. What was the result? Who knows? They didn't say. Although the fines for broadcasting VNRs are up to $32,500 per violation. Note the use of the words "up to." That means the fines start at zero.

Personally I don't believe paid placement is the root cause. The main culprit is more likely laziness. It's easy to file an article when all you have to do is copy and paste someone else's press release.

Sometimes we really do want to know the information contained in an Unpaid Placement Masquerading as Actual Article. I can't ever remember when the hell Ben & Jerry's free ice cream day is, but Mass Media always reminds me. Incidentally, go over to Baskin-Robbins the following day; they do the same thing twenty-four hours later. See? You wanted to know about that. It's hard to say exactly what makes Unpaid Placement Masquerading as Actual Article appropriate or not. I don't particularly care for ice cream but I damn well want to know if the local steak house has a half-off sale. If you're Hindu or vegetarian you probably couldn't care less. So it goes.

Much of Unpaid Placement Masquerading as Actual Articles is no doubt a result of the recent uptick in incidence of something called viral marketing. Viral marketing seeks to harness the power of the Internet to rapidly spread publicity from person to person. Standout examples of viral marketing are Terry Tate, Office Linebacker, for Reebok (from the Super Bowl commercial a few years back), the creepy-ass king from Burger King, and the undisputed champion, the film *Snakes on a Plane. Snakes on a Plane* accidentally succeeded in kicking up a firestorm of viral interest on the Internet, but it quickly turned this to its advantage by engaging "fans" (I use the term loosely, since no one had seen the movie) to make slight improvements to the movie, such as Samuel L. Jackson uttering the words, "Snakes on a motherfucking plane!" Interestingly, *Snakes on a Plane* was by far the most successful (and probably accidental) viral marketing campaign ever, but it utterly failed to translate into box office receipts.

Viral marketing is a double-edged sword, though. Take the example of Dear Emily. This was a marketing campaign for a show on Court TV that consisted of a fake person taking out a billboard to lambaste her fake estranged husband for fake cheating on her. It was submitted to several online Web sites, and sadly, we fell for it. Husbands and wives confronting each other via billboard has actually happened before, which is quite possibly where the campaign's originators got the idea. In one particular case, a series of huge posters were erected along a stretch of highway in Britain over the course of a week, consisting of one accusation after another from both members of a failed marriage. For all I know, that was fake too, but I never heard anything about it. At any rate, the Dear Emily billboard had a corresponding Web site with a fake blog with two weeks of fake posts and some fake video. The best part about the whole thing was that it was a viral campaign for a show on Court TV, it got national exposure for a few days, and I can't remember the name of the show.

The Internet filled with rage when it was discovered that this was all an ad campaign. It was the source of discussion for at least three solid days on many popular blog sites, and also received some significant media coverage from Mass Media. Was this campaign a success? I would argue it was not—the show was unsuccessful. This was bad publicity.

People claim that there is no such thing as bad publicity, but this is certainly not true. Just ask Michael Jackson. Or Marv Albert. Or Kobe Bryant. Or Milli Vanilli. Or Tom Cruise. Bad publicity can do some serious and permanent damage to reputations. It can end careers, or as happened in the case of Dear Emily, it can end entire TV series. People were so angered with the deception that the show was permanently tainted with the stigma of sucking out loud.

The particular articles covered in this chapter are fairly minor issues, without a doubt. For example, who honestly gives a crap about vegetables being consumed during the Super Bowl? The reason the examples are important is because people read these articles and believe them to be 100 percent true based solely on the fact that it was heard on the radio, read in the newspaper, seen on the TV, or browsed on the Internet. As far as journalists are concerned, the actual news here is that someone else said something. "Someone says that veggies are the top Super Bowl snack" should be the real headline. They will argue that readers can tell the difference between repeated comment and actual news. It turns out they can't and don't and won't. Readers assume information carried by Mass Media is true solely because it appears there. While Mass Media asks its audience to treat all media matters with a degree of skepticism, no one actually does. People expect Mass Media to do that for them, but it doesn't. Whether it should is another issue entirely.

Mass Media should at least take into account the fact that people don't have the time or the volition to question everything they read and change their editorial decisions accordingly, instead of hiding behind the claim that we should all know better.

Headline Contradicted by Actual Article

WE LIVE IN A PRETTY BORING WORLD FOR THE MOST PART. AR-chaeologists don't flee rolling boulders while carrying priceless statues, chemists don't blow things up all the time, and teachers often fail to make a difference in most students' lives. This lack of excitement is problematic for the lazy journalist, who can't get people excited about the mundane everyday events that make up the majority of life. As a result, sometimes they're forced to punch up events to make them more interesting.

Journalists are traditionally taught to find an angle on a story. It's hard to argue with that, considering that just reading a straight-up retelling of events is pretty dull. The angle is what gets us interested and makes us want to continue reading. Problems occur, however, when the journalist has to find an angle on a story that doesn't really have one.

There are three main ways that Headline Contradicted by Actual Article examples see print. The first culprit is that no one catches the contradiction between the article and the headline. Good journalists stay pretty busy; sometimes they just miss things. It happens.

The second, somewhat less likely source is a journalist's doing an interview, mishearing something, and then writing the article. Journalists get all worked up because they think they are hearing fairly groundbreaking news but later find out that the main thrust of the article isn't true at all. Still, they have a deadline to meet. So they bury the real conclusion several paragraphs down, leave for the day, and hit the local watering hole.

The third cause of Headline Contradicted by Actual Article is that many of these articles are written with the journalist's full knowledge that the headline is misleading, but they use the real conclusion as the "twist" to get your attention toward the end. Many scientific studies, for example, are victims of overexaggeration by zealous writers trying to punch up their stories.

SCIENTISTS TEST 118-YEAR-OLD DNA, DETERMINE THERE'S A GOOD CHANCE IT WAS ACTUALLY "JILL THE RIPPER."

Actual headline: DNA Hints at Jill the Ripper.

Actual article: The test was inconclusive, and furthermore this article should have been about the testing procedure and not a different, overhyped conclusion.

Now, here's an interesting claim. It turns out that an Australian professor found some DNA samples on the back of postage stamps on letters mailed from Jack the Ripper. He tested it and discovered that the person who licked the stamps was actually female. Wow, this really *is* news! All this time we've been thinking it was Jack the Ripper but really it was Jill the Ripper. This turns everything we thought we knew on its head.

Except that in the fourth paragraph, there's the following actual quote from the professor who did the testing: "It's possible the Ripper could be female but the results are inconclusive.... He said because the samples were so old, very small and poorly preserved, only a partial profile was built that 'didn't reach forensic standards' nor identified an individual."

Now, wait a damn minute. The headline says it was Jill the Ripper. The first paragraph implies that as well. Then for the remainder of the article, we have nothing but paragraph after paragraph telling us that the DNA evidence is incomplete and there's no way to tell. Man, that's a hell of a disappointment.

It turns out the actual article was an interview with the professor, who was talking about a new forensic technology he'd developed. No doubt the reporter was nodding off in his chair until the professor mentioned Jill the Ripper.

» ScottMpls

I read that as "Jill the Stripper." Disappointing.

» LegacyDL

Jack and Jill The Ripper were a well known Victorian BDSM sibling duo. The only reason their "clients" died was because they forgot the safe word.

» Uncoveror

A little tidbit on historical revisionism: You aren't going to get published by repeating what is generally accepted. You have to claim something new and different to get into print. It is the same whether you are writing a master's thesis, a doctorial dissertation, a book or a news article. View any revisionist claim with a healthy sense of skepticism.

» Alhazred

Regardless, this "partial profile" only says it "might" be a woman. Ergo, it might be a man.

DRACULA'S CASTLE TAKEN OVER BY THE HAPSBURGS.

Actual headline: Dracula Castle to Be Returned to Owner.

Actual article: It's not really Dracula's castle and we're not sure he ever even visited it.

You may or may not recall that godless commie heathens took over Romania in the late 1940s. It happened to quite a few Eastern European countries, couldn't really be helped. In the process of liberating possessions and property from the bourgeois capitalist pigs, the owners of Dracula's Castle were given the boot.

Fast-forward sixty years. Communism is gone because they couldn't pay their bills. On top of all of that, tourist money is a valuable commodity. For whatever reason, the Romanian government decides to give Dracula's Castle back to the descendants' original owners, in this case Dominic van Hapsburg, who incidentally is a New York architect.

Now, it strikes me as odd that Romania would just give a castle to some random guy for no reason; no doubt there is more to that story. Anyhow, they did give it to van Hapsburg, who I'm sure was very appreciative.

Then way down in the article we have this little gem:

> While known and marketed as "Dracula's Castle," the Bran Castle never belonged to Prince Vlad the Impaler, who inspired Bram Stoker's Count Dracula character, but the prince is thought to have visited the medieval fortress.

Now, the only reason anyone gives a crap about this article is because it has Dracula's Castle in the headline. The following day dozens of radio stations across the United States mentioned it in their morning show news roundups. No one mentioned (as far as I know) the fact that there was another castle nearby, Peles Castle, that was given back to its original owner as well, some guy named King Michael. They probably could have gotten some decent international press if they'd given it to Pelé by mistake, but odds are he owns too many castles already to take in another one.

So there you have it. Headline: Dracula's Castle Given Back to Original Owners. Article: Dracula never lived there, although we think he visited there once. Great. On the off chance you go there and are disappointed by this fact, you could always cheer yourself up by visiting the nearby Dracula theme park. If it had ever gotten built, which it hasn't, thanks to stupid environmentalists and Prince Charles butting in where he wasn't needed. Thanks for nothing, Prince Charles.

» Catzies

I discovered in my genealogy research that my family are Romanian and illegitimate Hapsburgs to boot.

get outta my castle you kids

» Adman12

But before you collect your inheritance, don't you have to spend the night?

Just don't forget the Scooby Snacks.

The Fark tagline gives away the joke here....

ACTUAL HEADLINE: CBS NEWS TO BE "700 CLUB" OF GAY NEWS

First line of article: "We don't want to be the '700 Club' of gay news."

Yup, that was the first line of the article.

CBS News apparently decided to launch a version of its evening news on the Logo channel. Logo, by the way, is a gay and lesbian cable network. I had never heard of it, but I live in a red state; for all I know, it's hugely popular elsewhere (but I doubt it). The article doesn't say how long the news segment is, but it does say it runs the 3-to-5-minute segment thirty times a day.

Courtland Passant, executive producer for the CBS news segment, says in the article that the segment will center on gay issues but doesn't want to appear to be pandering (hmmm) to a gay audience. Passant goes on to say that because they're dealing with gay issues, they don't need a counterpoint conservative view to any issues featured on the show. This may come as a shock to you, but it turns out that conservatives are likely against all the gay issues that will be covered, so why waste anyone's time pointing out the obvious?

The article goes on to get a few quotes from Jason Bellini, evidently the anchor of the show. No word on why they even talked to this guy, because his primary function is to read a teleprompter. That's it. It's not like he runs the cameras during commercials, helms the network as an executive, or even mops floors when CBS News on Logo is not on the air. Bellini says that just because CBS has a gay news show does not mean it has taken up gay causes. Now, there's a statement sure to piss off gays and at the same time not to be believed by conservatives. It also makes for a great Out-of-Context Celebrity Comment: Pretend not to support your core audience. They love that.

So where the hell did the headline come from? The article isn't about CBS News at all, it's about a show called CBS News on Logo. It's more fun for the article to pretend that CBS is under the thumb of the homosexual conspiracy. You know, those guys are in charge of everything, running the world from their shadowy gay hideout. No word on how the Jewish conspiracy feels about this. I'm already imagining *West Side Story* fights in the streets of New York with shirtless guys versus bearded men with long coats set to techno music with impeccable choreography. At any rate, I blame the conspiracy, whichever one it is that I'm supposed to blame for stuff I don't like. Someone let me know who wins the fight.

RANDOM ACTS OF KINDNESS: DARWIN HELPS CELL PHONE ADDICTS CUT THEIR CALLS SHORT DURING THUNDERSTORMS, SAY DOCTORS WHO APPARENTLY HAVE A DEEP UNDERSTANDING OF WEATHER SCIENCE.

Actual headline: Hang Up Your Cell or Get Hit by Lightning.

Actual conclusion: Being on a cell phone does not make it more likely that you will be hit by lightning. It will, however, hurt more.

This article would also qualify for Media Fearmongering, by the way. And Unpaid Placement Masquerading as Actual Article to a certain extent. Damn, this article rocks. It best qualifies for Headline Contradicted by Actual Article because, well, nowhere in the actual article does it claim that talking on a phone makes you more likely to be hit by lightning. Nowhere. On top of that, someone's trying to make a buck off this bogus conclusion.

My friend Andrea is deathly afraid of thunderstorms. She has a good reason, though; she's almost been hit by lightning eight times. It takes her about ten minutes to recount all the stories for each time it happened. I'll cut her some slack on that one. If anyone has reason to be afraid of being hit by lightning, it's her. For the rest of us, though, in reality it's highly unlikely that we'll get hit by lightning. It's even more unlikely that you'll get hit by lightning while on a cell phone. But that's not what this article would have you believe.

For whatever reason, a British doctor and her colleagues decided to write the *British Medical Journal* to warn of the dangers of getting hit by lightning while talking on a cell phone. I sincerely hope this plan was concocted after a long night at the pub, but I'm guessing probably not.

According to the article, their letter to the journal was prompted by a case in England in which a fifteen-year-old was hit by lightning while talking on a cell phone. The problem with this, according to the article, has to do with how electricity is conducted. Human skin has a high resistance to electricity, which allows most people to survive being hit by a bolt of electricity with a temperature hotter than the sun. There's even a term for this, *flashover.* The danger of using a cell phone is that it disrupts the flashover and increases the odds of internal injuries. How? I have no idea, the article doesn't say. Let's assume for the moment that they're right.

It certainly doesn't seem like a good idea to be hanging out in a thunderstorm with a metal object pressed up against your head. However, the doctors point out that they know of three people IN THE ENTIRE WORLD that have been hit by lightning while on a cell phone. Now, wait a goddamn minute. The headline of the article is: Hang Up Your Cell or Get Hit by Lightning. It even has a subtitle that says: Don't use your phone outdoors in a storm, doctors warn. These guys go through all the trouble to write a medical journal warning against doing something that for all they know has happened to only three people. Ever. Even worse, Mass Media jumps on it like it's some kind of pandemic and adds the claim that it makes you *more* likely to be hit by lightning. That will certainly increase news Web site traffic.

Incidentally, less than a week after this original article came out, some poor bastard in Colorado got hit by lightning while listening to his iPod. So it goes.

» Torch

What horseshiat. She was a teenager outside in a thunderstorm . . . in a park under a tree. I did not know you could be such a moran and call yourself a doctor.

» Robhead

It's not about being right, it's about getting published: "Esprit and other doctors at the hospital added in a letter to the British Medical Journal . . ."

» I_am_jesus

yeah, i call bullshiat too. Lightning seeks out a ground.
   ground (n): a seemingly infinite supplier or accepter of free electrons.
   Cellphone = isolated miniscule bank of electrons. Just because it has electronics in it doesnt mean its any more likely to get struck by lightning.
   Correlation is not causation.

» Robhead

The doctor was saying that holding a metal object makes the injuries worse when struck by lightning (there is more metal in my belt buckle than in my cellphone), but the author of the story seemed to infer the causation, much asshattedness going on here.

» Major Thomb

This sounds likes some Internet chain letter.

» Jlop985

Being outside during a thunderstorm probably increases your chances of getting hit more than a cell phone can ever do.

» Mt_Honkey

The fraction of people using a cell phone during a storm has to be tiny compared to holding other metal objects such as, say, a watch. Science should not be done via press release.

» Imfallen_angel

Did she gain any super-powers over this?

» Rapmaster2000

Not nearly enough attention is being paid to the dangers of talking on a cell phone while driving with an alligator on your lap. What if the airbag went off?

» Moel

Ah-ha but here's an interesting piece of information gleamed from the BBC websites version of this story

The odds of being struck by lightning are 1 in 3 million. Therefore if 3 million people are hit by lightning statistically one of them will be you!

/same logic as the rest of this article i figure

FARK HEADLINE: "PUBLIC SCHOOLS DO AS GOOD AS PRIVATE ONES." PRESUMABLY THE GRADUATES OF PUBLIC SCHOOLS SEE NOTHING WRONG WITH THIS HEADLINE COMPOSITION.

I really can't take credit for this one. It's not as if I'm the world grammar champion myself. I grew up in Kentucky, after all. In junior high, we learned some pretty outdated grammar rules, such as drilling us over the difference between *teach* and *learn*. Example: I'm going to _____ you a lesson you'll never forget. I'm going to go out on a limb here and guess that the kids in Massachusetts probably didn't cover the same material. There were also lessons on the difference between *don't* and *doesn't*. Example: He _____ want to go to the store. *Did* and *done* came up as well, although this was slightly more complicated because the issue was the usage in phrases like "he did finish" as opposed to "he done finished." I remember being just as boggled as the rest of the class as to why this was being taught, although it was also my favorite part of eighth-grade English because it was so damn easy.

The Fark tagline pretty much covers it. Testing indicated that private school students were ahead of public school students only in eighth-grade reading. The study also found that conservative Christian schools lagged behind public schools in eighth-grade math. My guess would be the difference is due to math problems such as: How old is this 50-million-year-old dinosaur? Answer: Just over six thousand years old and it was never alive since God planted it in the ground for scientists to find later. *BZZT.* Wrong answer.

Interestingly, the study itself comes with a disclaimer about its limitations. The article even mentions this, saying the study warned against its "modest utility." Whatever that means, the article doesn't go into details. Presumably the author wasn't too concerned with small details like "the conclusions not being entirely accurate or useful" once he was done writing the article. That, however, didn't stop the head of the National Education Association from claiming victory when asked for a quote for the article. He said that the research showed that public schools were "doing an outstanding job." Glad to hear all problems with public schools are solved on the basis of a study that warns it may not really indicate that conclusion. Leave it to politicians to jump the gun.

» Phospodar

Gooder. It's gooder!

» Bufu

Good, gooder, goodest.
  Public, publicker, publickest!
  /product of public education system, K–12 and college.

» SSPinkerton

This has been true for years. the fact of the matter is, most people don't send their kids to a private school to get them a better education, they send them there to keep them away from "undesirables."

» Whitefalcon79

It seemed like a perfectly cromulent headline to me.

» BlindMan

Assessing based on standardized test scores is kind of deceptive . . . since most public schools do only one thing well, and that's train kids to take standardized tests.

One culprit of Headline Contradicted by Actual Article is writers' creep, a term I've just made up on the spot to denote how the thrust of an article can change as it's being written. Fiction writers talk about how their story evolves as they write, that characters who were slated to die in the plot initially end up living and vice versa. In the media world, journalists start researching a story with certain preconceived notions. Sometimes these are biases but most often they are just general vague first impressions about the subject at hand. These impressions are later altered by the information the journalist uncovers through research. Headline Contradicted by Actual Article is likely caused by one of two results of writers' creep. Either the journalist ends up with a different conclusion in his article and forgets to change the original headline or, and this is the cynic in me speaking, the journalist is completely unaware that changes to the article over time accidentally end up contradicting the actual headline.

Another possibility comes from the source of many of the problems in Mass Media: a disconnect between journalist and editor. Some journalists aren't allowed to write headlines; this job is left up to the editor. Editors aren't always the most careful readers in the world despite what the title "Editor" signifies. Headline Contradicted by Actual Article is sometimes caused by an editor who reads an article too quickly and doesn't quite grasp the concept, or by an editor who is just plain stupid and doesn't understand the article for whatever reason. This results in an editor giving the article a contradictory headline.

The main problem with Headline Contradicted by Actual Article is that most people don't read articles, they read only headlines and move on. Judging from click-out patterns on Fark, the average person on a given visit to Fark will click on maybe three links out of around two hundred. As for the rest of the links, they read the outrageous tagline, figure they know what the rest of the article says, and move on. Oftentimes taglines on Fark don't exactly represent the article they link to, but then again, Fark isn't a news source either. We're just screwing around.

Headlines like "Kentucky Wins NCAA Championship, Duke Sucks" are pretty self-explanatory; you already know what the article is about without reading it. There's certainly nothing wrong with this; sometimes it's impossible to make up a headline that would compel any noninterested party to read the article. It's the nature of the business. But real problems occur when articles with headlines making false claims see print. They run the very real risk of being taken seriously by the reading public.

We can give Mass Media a pass on this one, because it's highly unlikely they realize they're running Headline Contradicted by Actual Article until it's too late. Mistakes happen for whatever reason and often can't be helped. This is in direct contrast to Equal Time for Nutjobs, where editorial is often well aware that the subject matter of the article is complete and utter crap, yet they still run the story....

Equal Time for Nutjobs

THE MEDIA PATTERN OF EQUAL TIME FOR NUTJOBS TAKES ITS name from the fact that, for whatever reason, Mass Media feels compelled to insert "alternate viewpoints" into scientific articles from people who are obviously complete loons. If we're talking about a debate over, say, the best way to make a fuel-efficient vehicle, by all means go out and find other viewpoints. Alternate viewpoints are very important to scientific discussions. Political discussions too. But Mass Media is also fond of taking an issue that is obviously not up for debate and finding some nutball with no credentials to make a counterpoint.

You've probably noticed, for example, that just about any time the media runs an article about the moon landings, they have to give at least a paragraph to the people who think Neil Armstrong was a paid actor who moonwalked on a Hollywood back-lot sound stage. Or that coverage of Holocaust deniers often initially fails to point out that the question of whether it actually happened isn't actually in doubt. Ever wonder why we've even heard of tinfoil hats blocking out mind-control rays? Because some nutjobs actually believe it, and somewhere along the way Mass Media gave them press coverage. Writers usually double back to mention later in the article that these people are indeed nutjobs, but then why mention it in the first place? I'm not talking about urban legends here, I'm talking about established events that no one doubts. Except for the nutjobs.

Equal Time for Nutjobs is really just an extension of equal-time treatment of political issues, but taken one step too far. Certainly if we're talking about abortion or gay rights for whales we want to hear both sides of the story. The failure occurs when the same treatment is applied to scientific principles. I realize that there are quite a few scientific questions that are not cut-and-dried, but come on, there was a moon landing, AIDS isn't an engineered disease, and the Loch Ness Monster doesn't exist. Among other things.

SCIENTICIAN SAYS SATELLITE PHOTOGRAPHS INDICATE THAT NOAH'S ARK IS ON TOP OF MT. ARARAT. WITH VAGUE PIC GOODNESS AND CNN'S "CRITICAL" ANALYSIS OF SAID CLAIM.

One of the issues slightly off the nutjob radar is that of the final resting place of Noah's Ark. Despite the fact that there is no scientific evidence whatsoever of a great flood that killed off nearly all the animal life on the planet except for the samples stored away on a large boat six thousand years ago, Mass Media continues to run articles about the supposed discovery of the remains of the ark.

Perhaps this is political correctness run amok. Perhaps Mass Media is afraid of offending religious sensibilities by pointing out that the planet is not six thousand years old. They certainly don't have any problem pointing out that people don't meet other people in bars to harvest organs or that Bill Gates doesn't really want to pay you to forward e-mails to your friends.

The only difference between bullshit we must have respect for and bullshit we can just talk about openly is how long ago people first started believing it. You say the Soviets invented baseball? You're a loon. You say that God tells you women should stay covered from head to toe, not be allowed to go to school, nor be allowed to drive cars? I respect your beliefs. P.S.: Please keep oil prices down.

From the article:

> Whatever it is, the anomaly of interest rests at 15,300 feet (4,663 meters) on the northwest corner of Mount Ararat, and is nearly submerged in glacial ice. It would be easy to call it merely a strange rock formation.

Yeah, that's right, let's not take the easy way out and call a rock formation a rock formation. Then we couldn't continue writing about this bullshit topic.

Here comes the nutjob introduction:

> But at least one man wonders if it could be the remains of Noah's Ark.

Funny how no one else does. Yet this idiot deserves an entire article on CNN somehow.

According to the article, the nutjob of note, Porcher Taylor, has some pretty big credentials. Turns out he's an associate professor in paralegal studies at the University of Richmond's School of Continuing Studies in Virginia, and has been a national security analyst for more than thirty years. Ah, but what does that have to do with archaeology? Not a damn thing, and the article sidesteps the issue. "I had no preconceived notions or agendas when I began this in 1993 as to what I was looking for," Taylor said. But somehow he still manages to see Noah's Ark in a rock formation.

The article does manage to give some equal time to a non-nutjob:

> There are also experts in remote sensing [using satellites to locate things, such as faces on Mars] who offer a skeptical view. "Image interpretation is an art," said Farouk El-Baz, Director of the Boston University Center for Remote Sensing.

Hey, it's a quote from a guy who actually has credentials talking about his own field of expertise. Whose comments are buried three-quarters of the way down the article.

This article is constructed in the classic "Bullshit or Not?" style. Observe:

- Open with a bold statement: Do Underpants Gnomes Steal Underwear?

- Interview a nutjob who thinks they do. Pump any credentials he may have, regardless of whether they actually apply or not.

- Discuss how scientists are "hiding evidence" and "unwilling to admit the truth."

- Then interview someone who knows what they're talking about who says the entire article is pretty much bullshit. "Not only do Underpants Gnomes not steal underwear, they don't actually exist."

- Finish by saying that even though this is bullshit, the original nutjob will keep on searching for "the truth." Or at least his own version of it. "Nutjob Bob intends to continue his search for Underpants Gnomes, no matter what the cost."

Incidentally, at least five different groups claim to have discovered the ark's resting place, which is probably why this ends up in the news so often—Mass Media is interviewing all of them.

» Lionel Mandrake

This only proves the truth of The Epic of Gilgamesh.
OMG!! Aliens have sculpted a giant loaf of bread on Mars!! What could this possibly mean, and why is the guvment covering it up!?!?!

» EvilEgg

You are obviously insane, it is very clearly a picture of a man attempting to have sex with a sheep that is eating a ficus plant.

NOW EVEN NATIONAL GEOGRAPHIC *IS* REPORTING THAT CRACKPOT STORY THAT NOAH'S ARK HAS BEEN DISCOVERED.

It's one thing when an article about Noah's Ark appears in Mass Media. It's a whole other thing when it appears in *National Geographic.*

In a follow-up to the previous article, a group called the Bible Archaeology Search and Exploration Institute (BASE) actually sent a team to climb up to check out their particular Noah's Ark sighting at the top of Mount Suleiman in Iran. They arrived at the top, took a bunch of pictures of what looks like petrified wood, and brought back some samples. The president of BASE, Robert Cornuke, says he's convinced that he has found Noah's Ark. This is before any kind of scientific proof arrives, by the way.

In typical *National Geographic* form, they managed to dig a little deeper than CNN did. Turns out there's a little bit of controversy between these Noah's Ark nutjobs and the ones from the previous article. BASE thinks Noah's Ark is in Iran, the other guys think it's in Turkey.

Two-thirds of the way into the article, we come across the inevitable "Not everyone is convinced by the BASE team's claims." There's a shocker. *National Geographic* interviews a geologist at University College London who says the rocks don't look like petrified wood to him. Another British geologist says that boat-shaped rock formations in the Middle East are completely natural. He also points out that there don't seem to be any human-made joints or even pegged boards in any of the pictures.

Finally, *National Geographic* trots out the most obvious piece of damning evidence:

> [Martin] Bridge, the Oxford timber specialist, points out that it would also be impossible for a boat to run aground at 13,000 feet.
>
> "If you put all the water in the world together, melting both the ice caps and all the glaciers, you still wouldn't reach anywhere near the top of the mountain," he said.

So what exactly was the point of even talking to these people in the first place? Doesn't *National Geographic* have anything involving real science to investigate? If the purpose of the article was to discredit these ark-seeking morons, leading with the headline "Noah's Ark Discovered in Iran?" implies that it really was found, especially when the headline appears in *National Geographic*. The actual headline should have been "Religious Nutjobs Claim to Have Found Noah's Ark; No Scientists Agree with Them."

Incidentally, a Farker posted a screen capture of the most popular articles on *National Geographic* that day. They were: Photo in the News: Cat Chases Bear Up Tree; Photo in the News: Mouse Rides Frog in India Monsoon; and Noah's Ark Discovered in Iran? Perhaps *National Geographic* is just catering to its core demographic: idiots.

» Bubonis

Does anyone else see the Virgin Mary in the remains of the Ark?

» Gsr2k

Why is it a crackpot story?

» BorgiaGinz

Because these morons are pointing at a geological formation and calling it a boat

» Fahkinell

Well, until they find it to have neat compartments for two of every animal, and a giant room for poo, they just found a boat, methinks.

» RadicalDave

Why would they need a giant room for poo? They'd just shovel it overboard.

» Dr. Frisbee

I still wonder how they got the dinosaurs on that thing.

» Executive Monkey

Sadly, I bet this article is National Geographic's attempt to keep its American readers.

NUTJOB SKEPTICS DOUBT NEW 9/11 PENTAGON FOOTAGE, SAY MISSILE WAS VISIBLE IN FRAME NO. 3.

A friend of mine had the unfortunate luck of standing near the Pentagon on 9/11 and seeing a plane hit the building. He's not a government shill, he's just a regular guy who was at the wrong place at the right time. That pretty much settles the issue for me. I won't get into the other arguments against this, such as the far-fetched belief that obviously incompetent government bureaucracies are capable of creating conspiracies. They couldn't conspire themselves out of a wet paper bag.

On to the article. Years after 9/11, the U.S. military agreed to release additional footage of American Airlines Flight 77 hitting the Pentagon. They did so in response to all those nutjobs that claim it was faked. Not surprisingly, it didn't convince anyone. I did watch it; you still can't see anything. I have no idea why they thought it would help.

The article leads off with a quote from a philosophy professor from the University of Minnesota Duluth calling the new video a "charade" and arguing that the thing in the video hitting the Pentagon was too small to be a Boeing 757. First off, they should just automatically confer the honorary title of "Nutjob" when you get your Ph.D. in philosophy, because you have to be insane to think you can do anything with a philosophy degree. Secondly, University of Minnesota Duluth is a sucky school. This is the best job this guy could get. Credentials indeed.

The article goes on to say that the nutjob response "baffled" U.S. government officials. But did they really expect this new footage would make any kind of difference? We're talking about people who have spent literally years earnestly believing that the

U.S. government or the Jews or the homosexuals or Baltimore Orioles fans blew up the Pentagon. No way are they going to watch a video and say, "Oh, guess we were wrong." That's like expecting the Pope to tell the truth when you ask him if God ever said anything to him. Don't try that, by the way; it'll probably piss him off.

The article then highlights all the other various nutjob theories, mostly pipe dreams about killer rabbits and Dick Cheney being a bad shot with a missile.

The real bafflement here is why the media even gives these guys coverage. Compare the two viewpoints. On the one hand we have thousands upon thousands of hours of forensic science, intelligence gathering, and contemporary media. On the other, we have none of these. The two viewpoints are not equally valid. We're not talking about a religious discussion here, we're talking about an actual forensic event witnessed by dozens of people. Just because a number of people believe something doesn't make it a legitimate alternative viewpoint. I'm not trying to evangelize here. If someone manages to come up with some new evidence, such as a warehouse where the government is keeping all the passengers from the planes involved in the attacks, a missile fuselage, or otherwise, I'm more than happy to change my viewpoint. I'd rather be right than win an argument. I'm not holding my breath on this one, though. If the U.S. government couldn't conspire a way to plant weapons of mass destruction in Iraq in order to save face, I doubt they're capable of pulling off 9/11.

» theoneontheleft

If we can't agree whether it was the US or brown people who caused it, can we at least come together and blame Canada? You can clearly see a kamikaze moose with a maple leaf tattoo in the videos.

» staev

That footage clearly supports collusion between the space aliens and the reverse vampires. Case closed.

» jonathanpatt

It was flight 77 that impacted with the Pentagon. My personal theory is that they are not releasing any clear footage to drive the nutjob conspiracy theories, so that when they eventually pull out all the footage that does show something, it totally discredits conspiracy theorists, including the ones that are actually on to something.

There is a conspiracy. This is just not it.

» All Apologies

Pfft, there are some conspiracy theorists out there who think that wrestling is fake.

» G-This 'H'

Seriously, don't let your hatred of the current administration lead you to create a far fetched theory based on blurry security camera footage to further uphold your previous claims of high level corruption.

All this does is show the world your knee-jerk, fact-ignoring outlook. The same kind of label you place on the Bush Administration.

/takes one to know one?

» Detry

I have evidence that my penis is a cruise misile and is smarter than most of you

» Torc

Well, you're partially correct. It is hollow, mostly for show, emits a burning discharge from one end, and everybody is thankful when it never gets used.

ARCHAEOLOGISTS DON'T LISTEN TO MAN CLAIMING EDEN AND ATLANTIS WERE IN FLORIDA, PREFERRING TO COME UP WITH THEIR OWN INSANE THEORIES.

Here's an article that is obviously complete BS. The article's headline: "Discovery Could Rock Archaeology." Along those same lines, so could proving that little people live in my TV.

Here's the lead-in: "A tireless prophet with a salt-and-pepper beard and an inviting grin, John Saxer knows that mainstream archaeologists, journalists and folks in Tarpon Springs think he's nuts." Oh, yeah, here we go, nutjob all the way. Perhaps the reason everyone thinks he's nuts is because he really is.

The second paragraph pretty much sums everything up:

> They reject his Greek mythology- and archaeology-based theories that Tarpon Springs is the center of the biblical Garden of Eden and the Tampa Bay area coastline was the seaport of Atlantis.

Wonder why that is?

It's hard to tell if the article is really backing Saxer up, considering all the snide comments slipped in here and there: "'It's been a tough sell,' acknowledges Saxer, a 55-year-old bicycle mechanic and bartender who was homeless for much of 2004."

The article goes on to say that recently a Real Archaeologist with Real Funding has appeared on the scene to back up Saxer's efforts to prove that some random rocks he found lying around are really 6,500-year-old stone anchors. Says Bill Donato (the "Real" Archaeologist):

"I don't believe any of the Garden of Eden theories, or most of John's views of Atlantis, which I did my master's thesis on," Donato said before his trip here. "I'm interested because the pictures are similar to anchors found at Bimini last year and to [5,000-year-old] finds in the Middle East."

Now there's a resounding endorsement. But it gets better. The article says that Donato is known for his previous work with the Association for Research and Enlightenment. As Farker Moonbat pointed out in the comment thread for this article on Fark, these guys are pretend archaeologists. The Association for Research and Enlightenment is a society to honor Edgar Cayce, crackpot psychic extraordinaire, who was one of the first famous channelers of fake spirits and an all-around nutbag.

There's a description of an entire day spent with Saxer and Donato when they wander around looking for rocks. This goes on for several paragraphs and is even less exciting than it sounds. They do find a few rocks that Saxer claims, and Donato agrees, are really stone anchors. Hooray. Rocks.

We get a brief respite from the insanity when the author slips in the following note: Roger Smith, Florida's state underwater archaeologist, said, "Stone anchors have not been discovered in Florida."

Now the article turns to the real experts, who get in some great jabs.

Michael Faught, a former Florida State University archaeology professor who worked alongside Donato at Bimini, said mainstream archaeologists rarely get involved with those yearning to find evidence of higher early societies or to prove biblical history.

"It gets uncomfortable getting stuck between nut balls and academics," Faught said. "I believe it's important to stay open-minded to new ideas, but there's a limit."

And these guys are well past that limit.

The author takes us back to Saxer, who continues to dig himself an even deeper credibility hole. "'The anchors are a link to how we got here on Earth,' said Saxer, who once designed a line of pyramid energy beds sold in stores."

The article itself has a comments section on its own site, mostly filled with people either reiterating different versions of "I believe" or attacking Saxer for being an idiot. For some reason, no one attacks the author for even writing this story in the first place. Articles like this should never see print in a respectable media source, period.

No doubt the Mass Media Web site, in this case Tampa Bay Online (*The Tampa Tribune,* WFLA), could claim that this article isn't really meant to be taken seriously since it showed up on one of their blogs. However, blogs shouldn't be considered to be *just* blogs when they're attached to a news site. That would make them Mass Media Sections That Update More Often but with Less Editorial Oversight instead. They are still creations of Mass Media and no less responsible for the content. And further proving my point, this article did see print later in *The Tampa Tribune.*

At least *I hope* less editorial oversight is to blame for this article seeing print, because otherwise there's no excuse for the fact that this article even appeared on a news Web site. Here we have a guy without one shred of evidence to back his story up, scientists lined up one after the other to point out he's a nutjob, and this guy gets a couple thousand words worth of media coverage with a tagline that seems to allege that his theories have some merit.

» Bicycle safety tip

I always just assumed Seaworld was built on the ruins of Atlantis, so this works for me.

» The Anti-Laura

I'm glad crazy is still something we can all point and laugh at. Sometimes I forget what real entertainment is like.

» MrPerfectSU

Quoting the article: "'I don't believe any of the Garden of Eden theories, or most of John's views of Atlantis, which I did my master's thesis on,' Donato said before his trip here."

No reputable archaeologist writes his master's thesis on Atlantis. I googled this guy's name to try and find his educational background but got nuthin. My guess is that he is only slightly more reputable than the crazy homeless guy that gave him the lead.

The only legit way a scholar can get away with writing a master's thesis on Atlantis is if they are focusing on either mythology or Plato.

If he turns out to be a modern-day Schliemann and discovers Atlantis, I will gladly eat my own poo. Call me when that happens.

» Olithon20

So Eden was a land of discount malls, theme parks and retirement homes?

» Veale78

Woohoo! I live right on the coast of what was Atlantis! I should start a t-shirt business.

» Pair-o-Dice

This thread needs more boobs.

IMAGINARY SCIENTIST CLAIMS A 600-MILLION-PERSON JUMP WILL END GLOBAL WARMING. DAVID LEE ROTH SEEN PUTTING ON STRETCHY PANTS, WARMING UP BACKSTAGE.

This article originally appeared in the Technology & Science section of ABCNews.go.com. Seriously. I'll just let that speak for itself and move on to the actual article.

Hans Peter Niesward, from the Department of Gravita-tionsphysik at the ISA in Munich, created a Web site called World JumpDay.org. Its sole purpose was to have 600 million people jump up and down at the same time on the same day (July 20, 2006) to knock the earth into a different orbit.

This article takes Equal Time for Nutjobs a step further and actually points out that Hans Peter Niesward really is a nutjob. Or more specifically, he's a made-up character. He's a creation of Torsten Lauschmann, an artist, filmmaker, DJ, and photographer (to me that reads: unemployed).

The Web site WorldJumpDay.org claimed to have just under 600 million jumpers registered for the cause, which is interesting because that would make WorldJumpDay.org the single largest Web site on the Internet. So we can assume that was completely made up as well.

The article went on to detail how members of Web sites you've never heard of, such as treehugger.com and madphysics .com (although now that I have looked at them, they are kind of cool), have been debating the effectiveness of everyone jump-ing up and down at the same time. The conclusions were that it pretty much wouldn't work; madphysics.com took things a step further, though, and worked out equations to support their con-clusions that this is complete crap. See, they have equations; now, that's impressive. It sounds like they're probably com-pletely kidding around, though, thanks to the final paragraph in the article:

One word of caution: The site (madphysics.com) tells those of us living in the eastern part of the United States to jump at 6:39:13 because we are five hours behind GMT, but that is not true in July. Because of daylight savings time, Lauschmann has a part of the United States jumping an hour early.

Yeah, except that Great Britain does daylight savings time too, so the eastern United States is still five hours off of London. It is, however, six hours off of GMT, which the United Kingdom isn't actually on in July. I realize no one really gives a crap about this. I point it out because it further highlights how neither Lauschmann nor the article's author was really concerned about getting the details right. At least Lauschmann could use the excuse that he was just doing this for fun. ABCNews.go.com editors not only are editors for a living but they saw fit to put this article in the Science & Technology section of ABC News right next to serious articles on semiconductors, astrophysics, and stem cell research. Yup, this article sure fits right in there, as opposed to their weird news section.

» Smeggy Smurf

Can't we just have a 600 million person orgy and three day drunk?

» Fatal_exception

I have it on good authority from W. E. Coyote that this technique will work.

» WGC_CPhT

Diamond Dave can end global warming single handedly.
   BTW, Sammy Hagar is the cause of global warming.

» Franksfriend

so let's say his theory works. How do you know it won't send us closer to the sun? Or hurl us directly into it?
   I'll jump anyway.

» I_C_Weener

This will work as well as anything else proposed. Maybe better, but we have to do it one hemisphere at a time, else we cancel each other out. And China has an unfair advantage.

» Fatal_exception

And then we could try to get all 600 million people to run in the opposite direction to the earth's rotation so we can speed it up and travel forward in time to see if global warming really happened!

» JRHoward

From the article: Niesward's theory has at least one major flaw: Niesward doesn't really exist.

How is that a flaw in the theory? Sure, the theory has many flaws, but this isn't one of them. All this shows is that it's not actually his theory since he doesn't exist. Do people even read what they write anymore before publishing it?

COULD ALIENS BE OUR ANCESTORS? A GROWING NUMBER OF NUTJOBS THINK SO.

The problem with phrasing a headline in the form of a question is that it implies the answer is yes. Could aliens be our ancestors? Average Joe is led to think, "They wouldn't be asking us if it was unpossible. Maybe they is our ancestors?"

The article opens by discussing a recent Raelian "Annual Awakening Seminar" held in Australia. Raelians believe we were all created by aliens and that someday they will return to get us and take us who knows where. If this actually happens, I'm staying put. No telling what kind of problems are going on up there that we know nothing about. "Well, you see the Zafnus are feuding with the Weedles over short supplies of Fnorg. This threatens the entire galaxy, but we're hoping they'll work it out." I'll pass, thanks.

In an effort to trickle in a little sanity, the journalist interviews an expert on religion and society who basically said these guys are nutjobs. "They stand up against the mainstream for a whole variety of reasons." Most of which no doubt suggest questionable intelligence.

Then they tackle the entertainment industry. Did you know there are aliens and UFOs in pop culture? Did you know that nutjobs who believe in aliens congregate on the Internet? Have you been living under a rock for the past sixty years? This is like pointing out that cable TV exists, or that air-conditioning is great during the summer. What the hell is the point? Other than to fill space, that is.

We do, however, get a more in-depth view of the Raelians. It turns out they don't like being called a cult, but then again who does, really? They'd rather be called a religion, probably for tax reasons, if I had to guess. Actually the religion issue is a complicated one in Australia, which is where this particular article originated. Australia, aside from being home to such famous celebrities as that crocodile guy, that other crocodile guy who died, and Nicole Kidman, is the very same country where a few years ago a group of silly people started a campaign to have everyone fill in "Jedi" in the religion column on their census forms. The idea was to get Jedi recognized as an official religion in Australia. By Australian law, if enough people fill out the same thing in the religion section of the national census, it automatically becomes an officially recognized religion. Seventy thousand people followed suit, which was enough to make Jedi an official state religion, but unfortunately the Australian government was having none of it. According to a press release from the Australian Bureau of Statistics, they decided to classify Jedi-related answers as "not defined." Well, it was worth a try, anyhow. The upshot of this is that if you know enough like-minded nutjobs in Australia, congratulations, you're an official religion. In the Raelians' case, though, they're going to have to get over that little quirk of killing themselves to catch rides on UFOs if they want to have enough members to make the census count.

Having more time to kill and space to fill, the article makes a huge leap and starts discussing famous nutjob Erich von Däniken of *Chariots of the Gods* fame. Von Däniken's books alleged that space aliens had visited Earth before, a claim he based almost completely on cave paintings and temple drawings that looked to him like spaceships. Well, that proves it then; case closed. He also claimed that space aliens built pretty much every major ancient monument on the planet except for the ones built by Greeks and Romans. Apparently, tan people have problems working out engineering without extraterrestrial help, but Europeans, on the other hand, are really good at it.

The article then wraps with another quick quote from the original honest-to-god credible professor stating that some people "seem to be vulnerable to some kinds of charismatic leaders." Thanks for that news flash. The article spends 90 percent of its total space talking to nutjobs, followed up by the final conclusion, which is that, no, aliens are not our ancestors and these people are nutjobs.

This article would have qualified for Headline Contradicted by Actual Article if not for the blatant nutjob subject matter.

» ArizonaBay

Actually, the idea that earth was seeded with life from an alien origin is not so uncommon, nor is it so unlikely.

» BadSpeller

I totally remember that episode of Star Trek.

» LittleRedVette

So, are the space aliens ancestors of the really smart people, or the really stupid ones?

» Yotta

How much did that author get paid not to mention scientology?

» C4n7 5p3L1 R 71P3

I think earth is a multi-colored egg that was laid by the pink bunny of the universe.

» FarknGroovn

Q: What is the difference between a cult and a religion?
A: About 2,000 years.

Why does Mass Media love Equal Time for Nutjobs? Because so do media consumers, probably more than any other kind of Not News.

I visited the offices of *Pravda* in Moscow a few years ago. Part of the visit to Moscow consisted of the traditional Russian "let's get the Americans drunk out of their skulls on vodka" ceremony. I don't remember much about it other than that the vodka was amazing and the room was still spinning when I woke up the next morning. Part of the visit also included an interview with their press corps at their office, where we talked about any number of subjects for hours and drank more beer. Yes, beer, not vodka. Beer is for the office, apparently. Vodka is for when you've decided to quit fooling around and get serious about your drinking, preferably not at work.

One of the questions *Pravda* asked me hasn't been asked in any media interview before or since: "Why do you think stories about aliens or ghosts get so much Internet traffic?" I said I hadn't realized that was the case. They laughed; apparently it was a well-known insider fact that aside from stories featuring actual pictures of boobies or that are about sex somehow, the stories that get the

most traffic are about the paranormal. I replied that I hadn't noticed. I had noticed, though, that any links on Fark about boobies
or sex get several times normal traffic. Nonetheless, *Pravda* as-
sured me it was true—aliens and ghosts are big draws.

Well, it is true. Even the clicks on Fark indicate this. And Mass
Media, be it in Russia or elsewhere, is well aware of it.

In theory, Equal Time for Nutjobs should be harmless. The people
being interviewed are obviously out of their gourds. The problem
is that a Mass Media mention gives them instant credibility. The
media audience automatically assumes that Mass Media wouldn't
give coverage to anything they knew was patently false. Giving
the Noah's Ark folks a soapbox gives media consumers the impression that perhaps Noah's Ark does really exist, when in reality
there's no evidence of a global flood and there certainly hasn't
been a local flood large enough to deposit giant arks on top of
mountains in the desert. Christians who don't like this statement
should pause long enough to consider whether these Noah's Ark
nutjobs are trying to take advantage of their religion, much in the
same way the author of the novel *The Expected One* is in no way a
descendant of Jesus. I'm not attacking Christianity, I'm attacking
people using it to further their own selfish agendas.

Equal Time for Nutjobs is exceptionally dangerous because,
as I've mentioned before, the vast majority of people read only
headlines. People have a reasonable expectation that Mass Media won't run wildly inaccurate headlines like "Discovery Could
Rock Archaeology." The headline implies that the discovery
actually WILL rock archaeology, and if you glance at the article
without reading it fully, you see that the discovery has to do
with ancient boat anchors. I guarantee you a number of people,
probably frighteningly more than we would like to imagine,

considering which state we're talking about, now actually believe that parts of Florida are littered with boat anchors from an ancient lost civilization, because they didn't read the entire article. Mass Media's caveat is that the reader needs to make the decision, hiding behind this claim as if it excuses printing what they know to be outright lies. Mass Media likes to throw up its hands and pretend that people know better. They don't.

I fully expect that when I'm a senior citizen I'll have to read about actual scholarly debates concerning the reality of the Holocaust. I guarantee you the first argument will be "We don't know anyone who was there, how can we prove it was real?" It's already starting; Iran held one in late 2006. The media needs to cut this crap out and stop giving nutjobs a platform to stand on. And don't give me the "where do we draw the line" argument. Just make a judgment call, already. I'm not saying Mass Media can know all of the time if they're dealing with a nutjob, but they certainly do know most of the time. Giving these people media coverage only helps to bring other latent nutjobs in touch with bogus theories they themselves haven't even begun to consider yet.

Journalists do a disservice to all of us when they allow stories to see the light of day that they know are bogus for the sole purpose of attracting eyeballs to advertisements. President Bush Molests Children is as much an unfounded news story as any of the examples in this chapter, yet Mass Media will avoid running that kind of article at all costs. When Mass Media gives airtime to nutjobs, it is just one technicality away from libel and slander, the technicality being that the subject matter often doesn't have a personified voice that can defend itself. It's the difference between printing lies about an individual and lies about an abstract concept. The main difference—abstract concepts can't file lawsuits.

Publishing 9/11 conspiracy theories libels 9/11. Publicizing

World Jump Day, unless clearly labeled as a joke, which in most cases it wasn't, libels astrophysics. If a story claimed untrue things about an individual, Mass Media wouldn't touch it. Yet because these types of stories draw eyeballs, bring in ad dollars, and fill space on slow news days, Mass Media can't bring itself to stop covering them.

The Out-of-Context Celebrity Comment

WE'VE ALL SEEN IT BEFORE. MEDIA INTERVIEWS CELEBRITY, celebrity says something outrageous. Hilarity ensues.

It's not really clear why these gaffes get reported as real news by Mass Media. It happens partly because there is real public interest in celebrities, stupid as that may be. *Aftenposten*, Norway's main newspaper, also owns a tabloid that has a circulation many times higher than the regular newspaper. It also has boobies in it. It would be curious to see what would happen to circulation numbers if *The New York Times* ran bare-breasted models on their page 3. Considering that industry circulation numbers on a whole have been declining for a while now, it's probably just a matter of time before someone tries it.

Mass Media can't run the same kinds of made-up crap that the gossip rags can. They could; they just choose not to for the most part. Something about integrity of the news and His Holiness Edward R. Murrow or something. I can't exactly remember what the deal is.

Take celebrity relationships, for example. Mass Media can't really report on hearsay such as who was seen with who, who's cheating on who, and so on, without losing credibility as a Real

News Source. They can, however, report on factual occurrences, such as weddings, divorces, births, and funerals. While they claim to stand above the fray as far as celebrity gossip is concerned, they do exercise a certain amount of plausible deniability from time to time. One way they get away with this is via Out-of-Context Celebrity Comment articles. Out-of-Context Celebrity Comment is not quite news, but it's not quite gossip either, and that's good enough for Mass Media as far as newsworthiness goes.

When you get right down to it, it's all the fault of politicians.

There are, for the most part, four main types of celebrities: Politicians, Actors, Musicians, and Sports Stars. In recent years additional categories have come and gone, such as supermodels, socialite heiresses with sex tapes, chicks with great racks. Some of these minor categories are still considered celebrities, some have faded from view altogether. For example, name a famous current supermodel who is younger than thirty. Back in the eighties, everyone knew several by name. It probably had something to do with the fact that there were no boobies on the Internet and all we had in the way of easily accessible boobie-tainment was the *Sports Illustrated* Soft-Core Porn Issue. *Sports Illustrated* likes to call it the Swimsuit Issue, but we all know what it really is.

Among the four main types of celebrities, politicians are adept at screwing up pretty much anything, especially things that don't need fixing. Politicians have set the media-savvy response curve too high for other celebrities. Politicians are used to being hit with questions on the spot. They have answers ready for just about anything you might ask them. They're actually expected to know something about current issues, legislation, international politics, and so on. Additionally, they have the skill and/or talent necessary to bullshit their way around topics they either don't know anything about or don't want to talk about. For example, when asked an uncomfortable question, most politicians will instead opt to answer a question that they weren't asked in the first place.

Thanks to politicians, the media has come to expect that all celebrities will also have canned answers for anything they might be asked. Generally, the media doesn't go in guns ablazin' with stem cell research questions for Brad Pitt, but they get there eventually through the course of the regular interview. Media interviews celebrities the same way it does politicians for the most part, which is analogous to the old Monty Python skit where big-game hunters (journalists) use bazookas to hunt mosquitoes (celebrities). Unlike politicians, other celebrities for the most part are not adept at dodging questions, tend to answer every question even if they don't know the answer, and often fall into traps when the media tricks them into talking about something they'd rather not discuss in public. It's kind of unfair really, except that non-politician celebrities are fortunate that they can cry themselves to sleep late at night in their mansions atop their giant piles of money. That evens things out somewhat, as far as fairness goes.

In some cases the celebrity in question is actually fronting for a charity or a special-interest group of some kind. Most of these organizations are well aware that they are way off the radar of the average person. To get more attention, they can opt to do ridiculous publicity stunts, like PETA does on an almost daily basis. My favorite PETA protest is the one where they have a half-naked woman sit in a fake cage out in front of venues where circuses are performing. Hooray for half-naked women. What were they protesting again?

Like it or not, we live in a world where people will pay more attention to what a member of a famous boy band says on a technical subject as opposed to real scientists, who in theory should know more about what the hell they are talking about. Some organizations seek to take advantage of this by having a celebrity rally attention to their cause. For example, the president of the United States probably doesn't give a rat's ass about Lou Gehrig's disease, but he sure would like to meet a Cy Young Award winner in person. During the meeting, the Cy Young Award winner has an opportunity to bring up Lou Gehrig's disease, and maybe the president will remember the conversation long enough to actually do something about it. Or maybe the president will just nod his head blankly and zone out into daydream space until the Cy Young Award winner shuts the hell up. It's a gamble, but it's better than no shot at all.

True hilarity ensues when a charity organization or special-interest group selects a celebrity spokesperson (or vice versa) who is dumber than a bag of wet cucumbers. Celebrities fronting for an organization are expected to know at least a minimum level of technical detail about their particular cause during interviews. When they don't remember or don't know in the first place, this reflects rather poorly on the organization.

Let's take a look at a few examples of the Out-of-Context Celebrity Comment.

CHARLIE SHEEN DISCUSSES HIS THEORY THAT THE WORLD TRADE CENTER WAS INTENTIONALLY DEMOLISHED, NOT ATTACKED BY 9/11 TERRORISTS. GLAD THAT'S SETTLED.

This particular incident didn't get much Mass Media coverage, which is probably for the best. I was running the Fark article queue the day this story came in. I passed over it initially. Then it came in again. Multiple times. All from blogs. When this happens, it usually means someone's trying to stir up a media controversy for publicity purposes. Normally I just ignore those stories, but I couldn't resist because even if this was an attempt to garner publicity, it was some pretty embarrassing publicity. Posting the article on Fark resulted in a sizable chunk of Mass Media jumping on the story. Nearly all of the articles on Sheen's comments felt the need to mention that he was the estranged (a word the media loves because it sounds like "strange") husband of Denise Richards and that he likes high-paid prostitutes. Seriously, back-to-back mentions. "Charlie Sheen, estranged ex-husband of Denise Richards who in the past has been tied to high-end prostitution rings, said today that" blah blah blah. No doubt the day poor Charlie Sheen dies, Mass Media will put that in the headline of his obituary. "Charlie Sheen, who frequently banged high-priced prostitutes, has died."

In his defense, Sheen's comments came during an interview on GCN Radio, so odds are the question came at the end of the interview while they were just filling time before commercials with the usual free association one finds on talk radio. Sheen said he thought the south tower collapse looked like a controlled demolition. He said he'd read that eyewitnesses heard explosions from the basement levels of the buildings. He questioned whether a plane actually hit the Pentagon and how George Bush was able to see the first plane hit the north tower. "It's up to us to reveal the truth," he said. Uh, OK. We'll get right on that now that Charlie Sheen has weighed in.

Charlie Sheen probably feels left out of all the political media attention his father Martin Sheen gets on a regular basis. During his stint on *The West Wing*, Martin Sheen, who played the president, developed a habit of making political announcements to the media just like his make-believe character did. If he's a character actor, that might explain the behavior, regardless of the fact that there's no real good explanation for why Mass Media would even bother to print his statements. He's an actor, not a forensic pathologist or civil engineer. Ergo, who cares what he thinks about 9/11?

At any rate, Charlie Sheen made his first foray (that I've noticed) into Out-of-Context Celebrity Comment by going on record that he thought 9/11 was a conspiracy, not a terrorist attack. No word on why he waited four and a half years after the fact to get around to mentioning it. It'll be impossible to nail the government now; they've had too much time to cover their tracks. Now we'll never catch those bastards. Is that guy who played Columbo still alive? Maybe he can track them down.

This article on Sheen, by the way, is a perfect example of the double-edged sword of context-sensitive advertising. The concept behind context-sensitive advertising is that advertisements should somewhat relate to the subject matter of the article. That makes a certain amount of sense. But when news organizations attempt to automate the placement of context-sensitive advertising, everything goes to hell. Context-sensitive ads are placed by a software program that attempts to read an article, suss out what exactly the article is talking about, and then post related ads on the same page. Here's how it should work: If the article is about how U.S. cattle are getting really tasty these days, context-sensitive advertising should place ads for McDonald's or Burger King.

This may seem like a sound concept, but I can't tell you how many advertisements I've seen for low airfares that appeared in articles about horrific plane crashes. Or day-care ads in articles about Catholic priests being sentenced to jail for molesting kids. In the case of our Charlie Sheen article, a Farker by the log-in name of phosphodar managed to grab a screen capture of CNN's Web site main page featuring a prominent link, right below the Charlie Sheen article link, to CNN Health, which asked the oh-so-pertinent question "Are you a sex addict?" This is why context-sensitive ads and content are a really bad idea. A note to Mass Media: Just do it manually. Software in general is dumber than you think.

» labman

Is there anything celebrities don't know?
  Where's Bono. Can't he do a charity concert for something like this?

» DeanMoriarty

Oh great. A greenlit 9/11 conspiracy thread. I'm getting no work done today.

» GrooveMonkeyZero

I believe 9/11 was orchestrated by the Quebecois in an attempt to sell more poutine. Prove me wrong. I dare you.

IN THE ONGOING BATTLE OF POT VERSUS KETTLE, RADIOHEAD LEAD SINGER THOM YORKE REFUSES TO DISCUSS ENVIRONMENTAL ISSUES WITH TONY BLAIR BECAUSE "BLAIR LACKS ENVIRONMENTAL CREDENTIALS."

When he's not touring with the band Radiohead, Thom Yorke is involved with several politically active groups. These include Fair Trade Foundation of London, CND, Amnesty International, and the Friends of the Earth. Fair Trade makes some mean coffee, I think. I've never heard of CND; sounds like some kind of congenital disease. Apparently if you're a real rock and roll celebrity, you pretty much have to belong to Amnesty International; it's some kind of requirement or something. I've never heard of Friends of the Earth either.

As of this writing, Friends of the Earth, whoever the hell they are, is conducting a campaign called The Big Ask, whereby they petition world governments to pass laws against humans intensifying climate change. So far so good, right? Well, Friends of the Earth has been bugging Thom Yorke to sit down and talk to Tony Blair about climate change. He may not have been the best choice for a spokesman. We'll give Friends of the Earth the benefit of the doubt here and assume that they chose Yorke because they know that politicians are more likely to talk to pop stars about climate change. Especially stars with more influence over the nonvoting slacker youth demographic than no-name boring scientists. But it's hard to imagine what kind of conversation Friends of the Earth thought Thom Yorke would have with Tony Blair about climate change. Let's try anyhow.

> YORKE: We need laws to stop global warming. I can't prove it, but these people I work with on occasion tell me it's definitely the case.
>
> BLAIR: How exactly will this get votes for the Labour Party?
>
> YORKE: Uh. So anyways, global warming is bad.
>
> BLAIR: Can we take a picture of us so I can get some votes?
>
> YORKE: Go to hell.

After some preliminary conversations with people Yorke termed "Blair's spin doctors," he apparently reached the conclusion that talking to Blair about climate change would be a waste of his time. This seems like an odd decision considering that Yorke, as a representative of Friends of the Earth, should probably have been seeking out a meeting with Blair instead of throwing his hands up in the air, rolling over, and giving up. Although odds are that Blair, once he had a chance to think about it, would have reached the same conclusion, specifically that meeting with Yorke would be a complete waste of time.

This particular article is unusual because it is focused on what is essentially a nonevent. News flash: Radiohead singer announces that he isn't going to do something. And this somehow became an article? Your guess is as good as mine as to how the hell that happened. In other news, I would like to announce that I have no intention of meeting with Jon Stewart of *The Daily Show* to discuss NAFTA. Now, where's my article?

» PegoTheJerk

What are you talking about no credentials? Tom Yorke has produced millions of pounds in plastic wrapping, broken jewel cases, paper jewel inserts, and scratched foil/plastic CDs. That's quite a track record if you ask me.

» HenryFnord

Environmental cred is like street cred, only the roads aren't paved.

» Mastethom

I refuse to discuss absolutely anything on Fark with anyone because no one here has any <Insert Political Subject Here> credentials. By the same token, no one here should discuss any such things with me either. I suggest that we all return to looking at boobs.

» EdgeRunner

Obviously, Yorke is holding out for Pat Boone to schedule a summit meeting between all of today's politically-inclined musicians. He'd only be wasting his genius by speaking at any other forum.

COLOMBIA ANGRY AT BRUCE WILLIS'S COMMENTS ABOUT ERADICATING COCAINE PRODUCTION. YIPPIE KI-YAY, MR. FALCON.

As I mentioned in the introduction, the Out-of-Context Celebrity Comment usually occurs toward the end of an interview when people are just free-associating questions to the celebrity in order to get material for their piece. During a press conference for Bruce Willis's just-paying-some-bills movie *16 Blocks,* some mental giant in the press audience asked Willis a question about the cocaine trade. Which was strange because the movie *16 Blocks* isn't about drugs in any way, shape, or form. At least the parts I stayed awake for; maybe something crops up in the last thirty minutes. What was the question? you ask. No idea, the article doesn't say.

At any rate, Willis responded to the question by saying that the United States should consider "going to Colombia and doing whatever it takes to end the drug trade." It is interesting to note that if you add the words "District of" before Colombia, the statement is still equally valid. Yes, I realize it's not spelled the same (however, I did have to look it up).

For some reason, former Colombian president Andrés Pastrana Arango decided to leap into the fray and make public comment on the incident. I'd like to put special emphasis on the word former. Read: "Not current." No word on who the hell asked him what he thought, much less why it saw print at all. Sure, maybe it was because he was the Colombian ambassador to the United States at the time. It's more fun to pretend that he just woke up from an afternoon nap, read the comments, then fired off an angry letter to the local newspaper to appear busy. Arango's response was that Colombia made so much cocaine because of the "enormous appetite for drugs, in particular in the United States and Europe." So there you go, the entire drug problem in a nutshell: There's a demand, so Colombia fills it. Which must make everything OK.

I'd love to see the media's reaction if, say, former U.S. president Jimmy Carter piped up on U.S. policy every time no one asks his opinion on it. Oh, wait.

In general, politicians love a good distraction more than anything else. It takes everyone's minds off real problems. It's the same thing in Colombia. In Colombia's case, the government is fighting a covert war against the FARC (no relation), their economy sucks, crime is out of control, etc. Much like the United States, except for that FARC part. Seeing an opportunity, President Alvaro Uribe decided to jump in and make a statement as well. He called the actor ignorant and arrogant, and said Willis's comments were "a shock to Colombia's dignity." Note that he didn't say Willis was wrong, he just said he was offended. I think that pretty much says it all right there.

A week later, Willis publicly apologized, stating, "I spoke to the Colombians, it's fine." All of them? Apparently so. No one complained again. And still every year an assload of cocaine arrives in the United States from Colombia. Glad everything was solved so nicely.

FINALLY THE BREAK IN THE CASE WE'VE ALL BEEN WAITING FOR: SOPRANOS STARS ANALYZE JUSTICE SCALIA'S RUDE GESTURE.

U.S. Supreme Court Justice Antonin Scalia is a devout Catholic. He attends church every Sunday (as far as we know). My understanding of the Catholic faith, which I've reached solely by playing $5 blackjack at Christ the King Church during Oktoberfest against drunken priests dealing two cards faceup instead of one (thus making the game a lot easier), is that going to church every week does not necessarily make one a devout Catholic. It does, however, make it easy for reporters to locate you, ambush you, and pepper you with inappropriate questions at an inappropriate time.

So it's Sunday, Scalia is with his family on his day off. He leaves church and is suddenly assaulted by questions from reporters who have been camping out waiting for him to come out of church. In particular, the reporters ask how Scalia would respond to critics questioning whether his faith would have any impact on his impartiality in court cases.

So far the media's looking like a bunch of jerks. Leave the bastard alone, it's Sunday, for Chrissakes. Then Scalia one-ups them, literally. There were several articles written on what happened next. The original article said that Scalia gave the reporters the finger. Shock. Horror. The article was chock-full of outrage that a Supreme Court Justice might (1) give someone the finger (as if this is some kind of unheard-of thing that no one does) (2) "moments after having taken communion" (because apparently some kind of no-finger timer starts right after receiving the Eucharist) (3) outside a church (apparently the no-finger timer has a distance requirement as well, because ostensibly God pays less attention to things going on a few blocks away from houses of worship). The main focus of the article, though, was Scalia flipping the bird. Mass Media danced up and down, pointed, and waved their arms because apparently they live in a world where no one ever curses. Having been in several newsrooms over the past few years, I find this extremely hard to believe.

The following day, Scalia issued a statement saying that he

hadn't given the reporter the finger. He instead had flicked his right hand under his chin. So everything was OK, it wasn't the finger. He even fired back in a written statement: "How could your reporter leap to the conclusion (contrary to my explanation) that the gesture was obscene?" Well, that solves everything. Case closed, the media could go back to covering real news. As if.

But no, everything was not OK. One of the reporters present said he heard Scalia say, "To my critics, I say, *vaffanculo*." The other reporter said she didn't hear Scalia say it. Let's be like Mass Media, though, and pretend he did say it; it's more fun. The word *vaffanculo* translates as "fuck you." As for the gesture, it turns out that in Italy the gesture means exactly the same thing as the finger. Unless you're from Sicily, where it means "I don't care, not my problem." It also means "you're lying" in Greece, "I don't know" in Portugal, "I don't give a damn" in France, Tunisia, and Northern Italy, and "no!" in Naples. I'm told that in the United States it means "there's something on my chin I'm trying to wipe off."

In the third (!) follow-up on the story, the *Boston Herald* began by saying, "Amid a growing national controversy about the gesture made by Supreme Court Justice Antonin Scalia..." There was no controversy. Most people found it kind of funny, but let's get real, the vast majority of US flip people off and say "fuck" on a weekly basis. In fact, that very same week the AP released a poll saying that 74 percent of Americans surveyed said they encounter profanity in public frequently or occasionally. And 64 percent said they say "fuck" ranging from several times a day to a few times a year. So to this I say, who fucking cares if Scalia flipped off two reporters pestering him outside a church on his day off? They probably deserved it for invading his privacy. I'd have done the same thing myself. Incidentally, I did three radio interviews that week, one in New York City even, and none of the radio shows had heard a peep about the incident. The growing national controversy was apparently limited to *Boston Herald* readers, the ones who hadn't died off yet, anyhow.

Mass Media loves stories that embarrass politicians, and they tried to keep this one going as long as they could. This is where the Out-of-Context Celebrity Comment comes into play. It's partly Scalia's fault, he gave them the idea. In his statement, Scalia said that the *Herald* reporters had watched "too many episodes of *The Sopranos*." Having no other way to keep the story in the news, the *Boston Herald*'s fourth article on the subject was a compilation of interviews with several of the stars of *The Sopranos*, asking what they thought about the whole Scalia thing. This article was a complete waste of space, because who really cares what some actors think. But it did produce some amusing quotes.

Straight from the *Boston Herald* article:

"It's not like grabbing your crotch, not that bad an obscenity," [Joe] Gannascoli (who plays Vito Spatafore) said. "But it's an obscenity. It's something you would do after paying a bookie, to your bookie, but not something you would do in church."

"It's not that bad, but I wouldn't do it to my mother. No way. Would I do it in church? These days, maybe. It depends if the priest was giving me the hairy eyeball," said Stoneham native John Fiore, who plays *Sopranos* capo Gigi Cestone.

"That could mean 'forget about it,'" Vincent said. "It means he just doesn't want to even talk about it. He thinks it's not worth his time."

Good thing the *Sopranos* actors cleared all that up for us.

SHARON STONE THINKS KIDS SHOULD GIVE AND RECEIVE MORE ORAL SEX.

Here's the out-of-context version of the article: Sharon Stone tells kids to give more blow jobs. If you're like 99 percent of the reading public and don't read the actual article, that's the impression you walk away with. Well, that's not what she really said.

It turns out that, like Richard Gere, Stone is an AIDS awareness activist (man, there are a lot of these guys running around in Hollywood). She says she always carries condoms with her to increase awareness of AIDS, so if you ever happen to see her out walking on the street sometime, be sure to go up to her and ask for one. I'm sure she'd love it.

"Young people talk to me about what to do if they're being pressed for sex. I tell them (what I believe): oral sex is a hundred times safer than vaginal or anal sex. If you're in a situation where you cannot get out of sex, offer a blow job. I'm not embarrassed to tell them."

That sounds kind of reasonable if you assume she meant nothing by it. If you like to wallow in false outrage, however, you can interpret it as Sharon Stone condoning date rape. Which, let's face it, is absolutely not what she meant. I'm willing to bet that's not how she actually said it either, that the reporter heard what sounded like something that could create controversy, and just ran that version instead. They do that sometimes. You may have noticed.

» Bearsfolks

Good advice! Where was she when I was a kid?

» Nickyhopkins

Boy, someone isn't washed up and saying things purely for publicity! It's almost like she has a really lame B-movie coming out that uses body doubles extensively in scenes marketers tell me are "hot"!

» wanago bob

"If you're in a situation where you cannot get out of sex, offer a blow job. I'm not embarrassed to tell them."

For what would that situation be—Stone cuts in line at the supermarket or a fender bender?

» John_Denver_Lives

I think I should receive more oral sex, but that hasn't gotten me anywhere so far.

» ExitKloie

Corrected headline.

[Amusing] Sharon Stone thinks kids should go and see her movie.

» Khaal

She's advocating offering hummers to people demanding sex?

I'll have to try that around the office.

» JohnnyCanuck

"Oh . . . and don't forget to take it in the face, little girl! Guys like that too."

» Betona

Can she call my wife?

Pretty please?

» Shadowspawn

I can't believe I just read that from a woman who said that the beaver shot was unintentional.

And it didn't even look that trim in the first movie.

» Alucard1191

I personally welcome our new oral sex giving and receiving overlords.

» Hdhuntr93

Enough about the children, won't someone please think of the adults?!? Why should it be only the children giving and receiving more oral sex? Grownups are better at it, too (usually).

» Richochet4

Richard Jenni said it best:
   Why do men like receiving BJs so much?
   Because it combines their two favorite things, having sex and doing nothing.

FROM THE BEATING A DEAD HORSE DEPARTMENT: SPRINGSTEEN DECIDES THE RESPONSE TO KATRINA SUCKED. YOUR DOG WANTS A NON-FLOODING HOME.

It's going to be a long while before people forget that Hurricane Katrina pretty much destroyed New Orleans. After which, the citizens of that fine city promptly rebuilt it in the same place, ten feet below sea level right next to the Mississippi. What could possibly go wrong? Again, I mean.

Springsteen's comments came during a concert he played at the first Jazz and Heritage Festival held in New Orleans after Hurricane Katrina. "I saw sights I never thought I'd see in an American city," he said. "The criminal ineptitude makes you furious." It's hard to tell whether this referred to New Orleans post-Katrina or New Orleans pre-Katrina, home to one of the most corrupt local governments in America. It's also hard to tell whether he was just playing to the crowd, given that he's never spoken out about his New Orleans outrage at other events. That I know of.

That isn't to say that there shouldn't be outrage. Several

months after Katrina hit, my parents went on a mission trip to build homes in Mississippi, a state that most people forgot was also heavily damaged by the storm. The area was still completely without power. This is kind of a reverse Proximity to New York City media pattern analogy (see page 236), but do you think for a minute that the media would have sat idly by if part of Brooklyn lost power for several months? I'm going to go out on a limb and say no. It would have been the lead story on CNN and Fox News every hour.

The fact that this statement made news isn't really Springsteen's fault either. He made a few offhand remarks at a concert, and someone wrote an entire article on it. For the BBC. No word on how the article even saw print, considering the BBC's reputation as a hard news organization. Next up: an entire article about how the lead singer for Oasis drank some water onstage.

» MuppetPastor

Step one to avoid a flooded home: DON'T LIVE IN A FLOOD PLANE.

» Wraithmare

Well, at that point I'd sue the airline. Can't even roll down a window to let the water out.

» SockMonkeyHolocaust

Well, I totally ignored it when all those other celebrities talked smack about the government's response but, man, like Bruce is a New Jersey everyman! He knows.

» Gilgigamesh

I was actually at the show, and he didn't assign blame at least not directly. He mumbled something about criminal incompetence; he didn't say whose.

» quiefNpea

News Corp: "Mr Boss, you heard about Katrina, right?"
Bruce: "What exit? I live near the ocean."

» Dialectic

Katrina is soooo 2005. Can't we all get ready for the next natural disaster that's going to occur when Miami gets destroyed by a tornado. Won't you please pray for the 8th Street Latinas?

WORLD-RENOWNED MILITARY EXPERT CHER PUSHING FOR SAFER HELMETS.

I don't think anyone out there would begrudge getting safer helmets for soldiers. Although I doubt anyone knew that they currently weren't safe. I sure didn't. The problem is, we have only Cher's word for it.

According to the article, Cher has donated "more than" $130,000 (which can't be *much* more, otherwise it would say more than $135,000 or more than $140,000) to Operation Helmet. Operation Helmet pays $100 per helmet to modify them so that they are better able to absorb bomb blasts. How does this work? Hell if I know; the article doesn't say. We'll have to take their word for it. It's probably cheaper than wrapping the entire soldier in armor-plated plastic bubble. It's definitely not cheaper than not sending soldiers over to fight wars, but I realize that's not the world we live in. So it goes.

The Marine Corps offers this dissenting opinion on helmet safety: "The Marine Corps has commissioned a study to determine whether to change its helmets but has said the ones Marines use now are effective." It's hard to argue, really; if you're standing next to something that explodes, it probably doesn't matter what kind of helmet you're wearing. Unless the rest of you is encased in one of those armor-plated plastic bubbles I mentioned earlier.

During the Iraq War (the second one, not the first one), the

U.S. military came under fire multiple times for not supplying soldiers with sufficient body armor. The military did have a policy of allowing you to bring your own body armor, however, which resulted in Web sites such as Ernie's House of Whoopass (ehowa .com, R-rated) sponsoring fund-raising drives to procure body armor for soldiers. It sounds like a joke, but EHOWA managed to raise thousands of dollars through word-of-mouth. They're great guys. At any rate, this may sound a little rough, but the primary goals of a military have never been to keep soldiers alive. The primary goal is to win wars. And sometimes the two objectives are incompatible.

It's hard to make fun of Cher in this case, since this cause arguably is not a bad idea. You have to wonder, though, how she ended up as Celebrity Spokesperson for Operation Helmet. Maybe it was a chance meeting in a bar or something, or an introduction from a friend of a friend. If we consider her fan base, it's probably better that we don't ask don't tell. But good on her anyhow.

» BassPlayinManiac

"To be able to use your celebrity for something that you really think is worthwhile is so rewarding."
you mean like putting out your own beauty products?

» Firefly212

Bah, I know she knows the military . . . I mean, did you ever see the video for "If I could turn back time?"

» Hilary T. N. Seuss

When I look to 70s pop acts for my military advice, I go with the one with proven service in the armed forces: The Captain & Tennille.

» Danger Mouse

Meat helmets?
Actually, if someone opposes the war, but wants to truly show support for

the troops, donating money for defensive armor is a pretty good way to put your money where your mouth is.

» Cup_o_Jo
Considering during the Vietnam War era Cher was like Jessica Simpson it's about time she said something. Although I am pretty sure she was replaced by a drag queen years ago.

» Gmstudio
What about helmets for skiers?

» MWeather
If using your celebrity to help the troops is being an attention whore, we need more attention whores.

Why does Mass Media treat the Out-of-Context Celebrity Comment as news in the first place? Who cares what Brad Pitt thinks about stem cells, or whether David Hasselhoff supports the current presidential administration? These people are actors, not experts on biogenetics or political commentators. Hell, for some of them the term "actor" applies only in the loosest of senses.

But some people do care. Therein lies the problem. Entertainment and celebrity gossip attract a lot of Web site traffic. On Fark it's the second most popular page on the entire site, the first being Fark's main page itself. I can only assume this is standard across the rest of Mass Media as well. What better way to attract even more traffic than to dress up an entertainment story as real news? Once Brad Pitt says something about stem cells, the story is automatically a candidate for science and/or technology sections of Web sites or newscasts.

Better yet, Out-of-Context Celebrity Comment snippets from celebrity interviews are a great way to generate interest to get people to read or watch the rest of the actual interview. When you read a bit from an *Esquire* interview with Lou Dobbs that piques your interest, you just might seek out the magazine to read the rest of the article. Online media sites certainly cross-pollinate. Witness, for example, the fact that Fox News and CNN will cover movies, by 20th Century Fox and Warner Bros. respectively, with news articles showing how they did the special effects. Never mind the fact that these days the answer to "How did you do the special effects?" is "Well, we used this here computer and drew them in digitally" every single time. Maybe they used a Muppet or two as well, but that's not all that common anymore. The point of the news articles is to let you know the movies are coming out soon and that you should go out right now and see them, not to inform the audience in any way. The same goes for celebrity interviews; many exist for the sole purpose of selling movie tickets. It doesn't matter what they actually say.

It is interesting to note that in times of serious news events, such as elections, wars, and plagues (imagined and real), the Out-of-Context Celebrity Comment practically disappears from Mass Media content. This gives some indication of the importance that Mass Media itself assigns to these stories—good enough for filler, and not much else. In this one respect, the Out-of-Context Celebrity Comment appearing in Mass Media is somewhat reassuring. If you see this type of article on a real news organization's Web site, you can be almost guaranteed that nothing of note is going on in the world. Personally, I prefer it that way.

Seasonal Articles

IT'S A KNOWN FACT THAT SOME ARTICLES APPEAR ONLY AT CER-
tain times of the year. The problem is that the *same* articles appear
every year. No one blows their hands off with fireworks in February, no one has snowmobiling accidents in June, and no one's
house burns down due to faulty Christmas tree lights in September. Except in some parts of the South, where people leave Christmas decorations up all year round. One cherished seasonal topic
from my childhood was poisoned Halloween candy. An entire
generation of parents and children lived in abject fear of someone
poisoning their candy, even though there had never ever been a
substantiated case. Urban legends were harder to debunk before
the Internet. Either that or no one wanted to debunk the candy
legend because it made for good copy. When I was about eight or
so, one of the local malls decided to hold a trick-or-treat open
house. They touted it as the safe way to spend Halloween, because no mall store would ever give your kids poison candy. It was
so successful that they ran out of candy before it was even supposed to open. I didn't get squat. It was wall-to-wall kids and
parents, and no candy. Talk about a Halloween nightmare for an
eight-year-old dressed as a sheet with two holes in it.

The local mall quit doing trick or treat a few years ago due to lack of interest. Either people realized that they weren't in much danger in letting their kids out in their own neighborhoods or the mall realized that no one was buying anything. If I had to guess which was the case, I'd guess the latter. Never bet on people becoming informed on a subject.

From the articles that follow, you'll notice that there is quite a bit of overlap between Unpaid Placement Masquerading as Actual Article and Seasonal Articles. This is mainly because most seasonal articles are press releases from consumer-interest groups, political-action firms, and/or businesses just wanting some free press. The subtle difference is that these articles appear every goddamn year without exception, as if we hadn't seen them before already. Some of these will no doubt be familiar to you; others will have faded from memory twenty-four hours after you read them.

AMERICAN COMPANIES TO LOSE $780 MILLION IN LOST PRODUCTIVITY DUE TO SUPER BOWL, ACCORDING TO THE "I JUST PULLED THESE FIGURES OUT OF MY ASS" SURVEY FIRM.

One of the worst offenders of the Seasonal (and Unpaid Placement Masquerading as Actual) Article pattern is the $X in Lost Productivity Due to the Super Bowl/NCAA Tournament/World Cup/Surfing the Internet at Work, etc., etc., article. These articles are invariably published by survey firms looking for some free publicity. They start by making an assumption that the average worker earns $X and will spend Y amount of time not working due to the sporting event in question, and then they multiply this by Z number of people likely to be distracted by the event. It sure looks like these numbers were completely made up. What is this anyhow, the number of total American workers times three hours?

Mass Media never questions the methodology or whether the concept is even valid to begin with. People don't spend 100 percent of their time at work actually working. They will spend X percent of time goofing around. In fact, in honor of the subject matter, I'm going to make up a figure and state that they spend 25–50 percent of their time goofing around. The actual subject matter of the goofing-around time changes depending on the time of the year. If goofing around at work starts to impact productivity, people stop doing it or they get fired. There's a finite amount of goofing around time. Thus, sporting events and the like do not cost any employee productivity.

I should write this as a press release and see if I can get that printed in Mass Media, no questions asked.

» Loabn
I read that as "I just pulled these fingers out of my ass" and thought "You and me both, brother."

» Mugato
Is this the same asshat who estimated a billion dollar loss in productivity when Revenge of the Sith came out? Whatever.

» VlagimarPutin
I recall seeing this exact same headline last year before the superbowl.

» Marcus Aurelius
Just think how much it costs when the CEO does it.
Come to think of it, CEOs shouldn't even get to go to the bathroom, the way they're paid.

» Caly

I wonder how much productivity is lost due to State of the Union Address drinking games.

LAWN MOWERS: THE SILENT KILLERS

This piece was also an Unpaid Placement Masquerading as Actual Article, but since it was seasonal it made sense to run it. No one gets killed by lawn mowers in September, apparently. Either that or everyone who is going to have a lawn mower accident in a given year has them early if at all.

The Johns Hopkins Bloomberg School of Public Health apparently could stand by no longer without warning us all that these machines we use to cut our grass have sharp spinning blades underneath them. Let's overlook the fact that JHSPH released this in late April and is located in Maryland, as opposed to the Deep South, where the grass starts growing taller than the trees at the beginning of March. If this article were to be believed, by the time it hit the media, everyone south of the Mason-Dixon line was the proud owner of at least one bloody stump.

The highlights: 80,000 people each year have lawn mower–related injuries. Doing some quick fake math based on what I suspect the current population of the U.S. to be, it would appear that your chances of being injured by a lawn mower are about one in a bazillion, assuming you ever use a lawn mower or have a lawn, for that matter. Most injuries occur to those younger than fifteen and older than sixty. That makes sense. The best part: The article recommends that no child under sixteen be allowed to use a riding lawn mower. I consider this to be great news; I had no idea they could start so early. My older son is three, which means only thirteen more years before his ass is on a riding lawn mower every day of the spring (note to self: buy a riding mower). It doesn't say whether it's OK to give a sixteen-year-old a beer to drink while on the riding mower. I think I'll just assume it's fine until someone says otherwise. What could go wrong?

The article also contains some real gems of advice for using lawn mowers. Most of which amount to "Wear thick body armor and make sure no one is within fifty miles of you while mowing." Likely these are the same folks who advocate putting children in giant plastic bubbles to protect them from dodgeball accidents. However, there are a few other great pieces of advice, including:

Never service the mower when it's running.

Do not use riding mower on steep hills or embankments.

Do not tow passengers behind the mower.

Now, that last one may seem fairly obvious but let me interject with an article from the Fark archives: Man Killed While Parasailing Behind Tractor. Nothing in the article explains exactly what happened. Apparently there was a tractor and someone was parasailing behind it. A gust of wind came up and snapped the towrope. The article itself is so sparse on details it actually has to spend two paragraphs describing not only what the hell a parasail is, but the difference between parasailing over land and parasailing over water. It turns out one of the two involves the use of a boat.

So yes, apparently some people have to be told not to parasail behind a lawn mower. Or tractor.

» Junior's shadow
  Silent killers, my eye. I'd call them noisy manglers.

» LEADER OF THE FREE WORLD . . . SHHH

Quoting article: "There is no reason anyone under 12 should ever be injured by a lawn mower," said David Bishai, MD, PhD, MPH, senior author of the study and associate professor in the Department of Population and Family Health Sciences at the Bloomberg School.

All that time spent in school just to study people getting hit in the shin by rocks while mowing the lawn. Lawn mowers can kill! be afraid . . . be very afraid! Thanks Doc.

» KingOfThePoopEaters

I am organizing a "posse" of armed, concerned citizens from my neighbor-hood to hunt down and destroy all of these death machines. We will not allow these monsters to exist in our garages and sheds any longer. I thank Tim Parsons for bringing this to our attention. This menace will be exterminated . . . at all costs.

» Metatronlord

My neighbor had an old manual mower. The kind that was a handle, with blades in between the wheels. It was silent, but the only way it would kill is if you used it like a baseball bat.

» Inflatable Jesus

Quoting the article: Store lawn mowers in area with minimal traffic and not accessible to children.

Uh . . . most people keep their lawn mowers in their garage, which is generally accessible to children.

Where do they want you to put them? The attic?

» HAL_Lives

WARNING: ANTHING THAT HAS A "BLADE" CAN CAUSE SERIOUS INJURY OR DEATH!

/there, that should cover it

» Jument

Hm . . . I don't think that really covers it. How about:

WARNING: ANTHING CAN CAUSE SERIOUS INJURY OR DEATH!

» Totl_newb

this is better.

WARNING: YOU ARE MORE HAZARDOUS TO YOUR HEALTH THAN ANY MACHINE.

» Cryinoutloud
WARNING: YOU ARE GOING TO DIE. GET READY.

SEASONAL FEARMONGERING: HIGHER POWER CONSUMPTION THIS COMING SUMMER WILL LEAD TO POSSIBLE ROLLING BLACKOUTS.

This article usually appears in the springtime, warning us of the coming hazard of summertime power consumption.

It's too soon to tell whether this is a true Seasonal Article. Its incidence in the media rose dramatically in the early 2000s after Enron conspired to drive energy prices higher in California by scheduling fake rolling blackouts. Finally, something the doom-sayers had been predicting for years had come to pass. No doubt they celebrated until the wee hours of the morning about being right. It was further encouraged by the massive 2003 blackout in New York City, which, it should be noted, was caused by cascading equipment problems, not waning energy supplies.

In this article, Mass Media warns that upcoming summer power consumption will be so high it's in danger of crashing the entire grid. They cite all kinds of facts, like how long it's been since new power plants were added, how grid capacity hasn't changed in decades, and how we all like to turn our hair dryers on at the same time while running air-conditioning units in the summertime. It's filled with dire warnings about how we'll first suffer rolling brownouts, then blackouts, then civilization will collapse altogether. Good times.

The article in question here fits into another one of Fark's Media Patterns: Headline Contradicted by Actual Article. The headline: Power Grid at Risk This Summer. Third paragraph: "The group said power supplies are expected to be adequate this summer." The entire article reads as though there's impending doom right around the corner, whereas all the quotes from officials pretty much say that demand is going up but things will be fine. Oh, and we should probably build some more power plants in the future. Advice which no doubt everyone will ignore until it's too late.

Here's the problem with blackout articles: Very few of us have an emergency need for electricity. Those of us who do, such as hospitals, police, military, and the like, have huge power backups. To the average person, the prospect of going without power for a short amount of time in the summer means one thing: no air-conditioning. The horror.

It is interesting to point out that there is a similar Seasonal Article that gets run in the fall to warn of higher gas prices during the winter due to anticipated increased demand for heating homes. Duh.

» Sharkroy

Dear Media,
   STFU
   Good day.

» CommiePuddin

You know, I'd likely welcome a week-long blackout. Such a forced disconnection would likely cause me to, I don't know, do something productive.

» Killershark

I don't know why this is a problem. I lived in Brooklyn during the '03 blackout and liked it. Barbequed in the backyard and walked over to see the dark skyline. Power outages are kind of cool until the food in the freezer goes really bad.

» Uncoveror

And lo, the air conditioning did cease and everyone got hot and sweaty. And lo, there was weeping and gnashing of teeth. And lo, in the evening all did sit there in the dark.

» Pope Joan

Good thing I'm running my computer off some old potatoes and some wire.

THE ANNUAL WASTE-OF-SPACE REPORT FROM AAA TELLING US THAT LOTS OF PEOPLE WILL BE ON THE ROAD THIS MEMORIAL DAY IS HERE.

Every holiday the AAA puts out a press release telling us that there will be more cars on the road this year than last. It doesn't really matter which holiday; they put out a press release for all of them. Except for maybe Halloween, but I wouldn't bet against it, because someone always puts out a press release saying that kids should wear reflective clothing and drivers should go no faster than five miles per hour in neighborhoods. Maybe it's these guys.

I don't think the AAA even tries to punch up its holiday traffic press releases. There's no need; Mass Media will just run them anyhow, as if it's some kind of news flash that there will be traffic during holiday periods.

Here's the format:

State that there will be more traffic on the road during an upcoming holiday.

State that gas prices will be higher as well.

Post some statistics on how many people will actually drive to impress people with big numbers. Wow, 37 million is a lot of people! Golly gee whiz!

Get a quote from someone at AAA saying damn near any-thing. Have them repeat the first three statements in quote form. "High gas prices and increased vacation costs won't deter Americans from traveling." No kidding.

Yammer on about international travel and what percentage increase in cars we can expect. Fill with more useless quotes.

Aside from the fact that this is a pretty lazy article to write (copy and paste mostly), the entire thing is one huge ad for the AAA. We're talking about an article that takes up several col-umn inches telling us something we already know: There will be traffic. What we really need is articles from the AAA telling us when there won't be as much traffic. Now, that would be news.

» JohnnyDanger

  Why do papers even publish crap like that? They couldn't do something more useful with the space—like selling ads, or make pretty borders?

» Sinto

  Who's going to believe a report published by a bunch of recovering drunks from Alcoholics Anonymous?

THE FAA WOULD LIKE TO WARN YOU TO PLEASE NOT PUT FIREWORKS IN YOUR LUGGAGE THIS FOURTH OF JULY.

"Flying and fireworks don't mix." That's the first line of the article. It is now impossible to take the rest of the article seriously. You can almost imagine your local TV anchorperson staring directly at the camera, pointing right at YOU, and saying earnestly, "Flying and fireworks don't mix." Then you fall over laughing.

I feel bad for the FAA. So many people fly nowadays that they end up having to deal with the entire spectrum of the lowest common denominator of humanity. The target audience of this article is people who walk past one hundred signs in security lines saying don't bring firearms onto planes and somehow not only manage to miss them all but also somehow thought bringing a gun to the airport was a good idea in the first place. It almost seems pointless to issue press releases like this, since the audience the FAA really needs to reach most likely can't read. At the very least, if they can read, they probably don't often comprehend.

The FAA warns that friction between fireworks can ignite them on planes. Does this really happen? If I rub two sticks together long enough, they'll burst into flames too, but that doesn't mean it happens spontaneously if I leave two sticks in my luggage. More than likely the FAA really wants to prevent what most of us did when we were stupid teenagers: taking the things apart, making one huge-ass bomb, and lighting the thing off inside a plane. That and the fact that some of the FAA's security devices can detect explosive residue.

To spread the word, the FAA has launched a national campaign, "Fireworks Don't Fly," *with an emphasis on Florida* because

fireworks are more accessible here than other states, said FAA
spokeswoman Kathleen Bergen.

No, the emphasis on Florida is because, for whatever reason, it
has the highest concentration of morons per capita.

Even better, the FAA plans to send special agents to fireworks
stands to ask them to remind patrons not to bring fireworks on
planes. Nothing like depending on minimum-wage checkout clerks
working in open-air tents to get the word out about your new flying
initiative.

The worst part about this plan is the fact that the article
states that in four years, the FAA has cited twenty-five people
in Florida for fireworks-in-luggage violations. The FAA is
spending time, money, advertising dollars, and manpower to
make sure that a yearly average of 6.25 people don't bring fireworks on planes. What a goddamn waste of time and resources.

The article also states that while it's illegal to bring fireworks
on a plane, you can ship them via FedEx or UPS. Turns out you
can't via UPS (but can through FedEx!). If you try, you'll discover
the hard way that it says in the fine print in their cargo contract
that they'll send over a group of guys to "beat your ass." In the
highly unlikely event this Fireworks Don't Fly campaign was
even remotely successful, the FAA effectively just foisted off its
problems onto private cargo carriers. Way to go, guys.

» Marty2000
  Any other day is ok?

» Shaun of the Dead
  Yes.

» Free Spool

Sweet, my flight's on the second and I am carrying a duffel full of m80s and mortars.

» BassPlayinManiac

"Friction can cause these items to ignite during flight, leading to tragic results for everyone on board."

Riiiigggghhht, sounds like someone is a little paranoid. thats like having a knife in the car and expecting it to somehow stab you if you get into an accident. honestly, it hasn't happened in the past, it won't happen now.

» Clownpenis.fart

Bah . . . alarmist nonsense.

Why, before 9/11, I'd fly with 18˝ mortar shells in my carry-on all the time. Once a whole bunch of us passengers had a bottle rocket fight at 30,000 ft. Good times, good times.

» Bhopper

When I was a kid I used to order right out of the Blue Angel Fireworks catalog and they would arrive via UPS right on my doorstep. In NY. Including Class B shells. Those were the days.

The "War on Fireworks" is such a sad turn of events—just one more liberty being ripped away from many of us. Here in NYC the police actually CONFISCATE YOUR VEHICLE, forever, if you're found to have fireworks in it.

Of course if you're brutally molesting a young child in your car you're free to pick it up after your sentence is served.

» STATICFREE

5 bucks says we'll be reading about some asshat and his escapades with luggage fireworks the day after.

FIREWORKS TRADE GROUP CITES "PEOPLE HAVING TOO MUCH TO DRINK AND PUTTING FIRECRACKERS UP THEIR NOSE" AS A MAJOR CAUSE OF INJURIES. FARK ANXIOUSLY AWAITS VIDEO EVIDENCE TO BACK UP CLAIM.

Every July 4th we get the article about how dangerous fireworks are. It turns out that sometimes people light explosive fireworks and they blow up in their hands. This isn't news to anyone who was a teenage boy. Back when I was a kid, we used to light off bottle rockets by the dozen. One particular time one of them didn't quite make it off the launchpad and landed in the pile of unlit rockets that we stupidly had been storing right next to the bottle. Hilarity ensued. Actually there's no point in going into it; you probably have stories yourself.

Just in case we didn't hear them the first time, and we didn't, the Consumer Products Safety Commission (CPSC) releases injury statistics every year on the Fourth of July. The commission estimated that 10,800 people required emergency room treatment the previous year. That's about one-eighth the number of people injured by lawn mowers every year, but no one's outlawing those. Honestly I was surprised to find the number of casualties was that low. Also of note is that the rate of injury has dropped 90 percent since 1976. Sounds like things are pretty much taking care of themselves.

In this particular year, the CPSC also held a closed-door meeting and voted to take a closer look at fireworks safety, and to possibly take a closer look at the laws to see if they might need to be tightened. Proving yet again that the best way to keep government funding is to look busy.

The trade group interviewed in the article actually did say the following about where all the injuries come from: "It's teenagers having bottle rocket wars, parents giving sparklers to two-year-olds and people having too much to drink and putting firecrackers up their nose." I don't recall ever putting fireworks up my nose, but odds are if there's any video evidence, it's on YouTube.com, right next to the video of the kid who tried to light a bottle rocket out of his ass but clenched before it took off. If you haven't seen it already, you can probably guess what happen next, and you'd be right. I recommend looking it up.

» Oldfarthenry

Happy July 4th, Yanks! Try not to blow-up too many nasal passages this year, okay.

» Stoiclawyer

Ok . . . hold my beer and watch this . . .

» Hisphrenic

Gunpowder+alcohol=A good time for almost everyone.

» Mouser

How much farking alcohol do you have to have in your system to think that putting explosives up your nose is a good idea?

RUNNING OF THE BULLS STARTS TODAY IN PAMPLONA, SPAIN, JUST AS SOON AS COMPETITORS GET DRUNK ENOUGH TO DO SOMETHING THAT STUPID.

Every year in early July, Pamplona is host to Spain's most popular festival: the annual running of the bulls. The festival began in the

late 1500s but received serious notoriety when Ernest Heming-
way wrote about it in *The Sun Also Rises*.

Can there be anyone in the Mass Media audience who doesn't
already know that once a year drunken idiots line up to be chased
by rampaging bulls? It happens every single year, and Mass Media is more than happy to rerun last year's article on how people
get trampled and gored every single time. We know already. But
wait, it gets worse. They get a week's worth of mileage out of this
thing. There's a whole three-part media cycle built around this.
(See the next two articles.)

» INeedAName

It has nothing (a little bit) to do with being drunk, it's that whole man v
beast thing. Which is why I like to wrestle cougars, and other cats of
unusual size.

» the_marq

Yay, it's time for the "it happens every summer news."
  Coming soon:
  —protests against bull fights and bull running
  —the town that has the big tomato fight every year

» ElPingino

Actually, I ran in 1996, and I can tell you that the Euros were far more drunk
than the few Americans I saw. The running takes place at 7:00 AM each
morning and most of the runners just stay up all night drinking. Each year
there are more injuries from tripping over drunk people than there are from
the bulls. Minor injuries comparatively, but definitely more.
  Hell of a rush; I highly recommend it.

» Thistime

i ran with the bulls last year and yes I got the horn. . . .
  \\wearing a spiderman mask in dance clubs and bars completely obliter-
ated was more fun
  \\running = scary
\\\three slashies for sleeping in the park

IF THERE ARE BULLS RUNNING IN PAMPLONA TODAY, THEN THERE MUST BE NAKED PETA PROTESTORS.

Speaking of crap that runs every year, this article is the second in the Running of the Bulls annual media cycle. As it turns out, there are people in the world who think that the Running of the Bulls is inhumane treatment of the bulls. Go figure.

Most recently, PETA has taken to protesting topless. Luckily for PETA, every year they have a fresh new crop of hot female college students who have no problem getting naked for their cause. This nearly always gets front-page coverage in newspapers and on Web sites, because hey, it's a cute half-naked chick. Nothing draws more Web traffic than nudity and sex. Just don't show any nipples, that would be really bad. Amusingly, while U.S. news sources won't show the actual nipples, news organizations in Europe, particularly Scandinavia, always run dozens of pics of the entire T&A ritual.

PETA has taken to sponsoring an annual running of the half-naked hotties, which they say draws 1,000 participants, which really means there might be a couple hundred. Thanks to this shrewd use of nakedness, not only does PETA get free publicity, but generally the articles will include a statement by PETA saying the entire thing is inhumane, blah blah blah. We know, we know.

In all fairness, at least the bulls do get to try to kill the people who are annoying them. They're on their way to slaughter as it is; at least there's some chance for payback.

» Jetcar

PETA appears to be turning into some sort of nudist colony.

» ChuckRoddy

Good. Takes the pressure off of us animal testers.
Everyone go to spain!

» NotANinjaJustABox

I like how they say it is a naked protest then they go to say no one was fully naked. Not that being naked really drives home any point what-so-ever but I'm fairly sure being half clothed is even less a point on the imaginary protest point showers list. Can someone please explain how being naked makes your protest more valid?

» Manfred Richthofen

If the bull runs over the protestors, is that ironic?

» Sentient

I never used to think much of PETA, but I think they're on to something with this whole "we're the group that gets naked in public" thing. If they could just drop the whole "don't eat meat" bit, I'd become a contributor.

TO THE COMPLETE SURPRISE OF NO ONE, MAN IS INJURED BY ANGRY THOUSAND-POUND BULL THEY WERE ANNOYING IN PAMPLONA.

The third Running of the Bulls article in the trifecta: Someone gets injured. Go figure; antagonizing half-ton animals can lead to serious injury. Happens every year without fail. I doubt there has ever been a running of the bulls where someone doesn't get injured. No doubt the media has this article prewritten in a drawer somewhere. Just change name, nationality, and age, and you're done.

The AP has taken to releasing new photos of the latest gorings every day, which immediately become some of the most clicked-on photos on yahoo.com's most popular rankings.

In this particular year, the AP actually ran an article about how on the first Saturday no one was gored by bulls. News flash: Nothing happened today.

» HotWingConspiracy

I'm sure sitting in a wheelchair for the rest of his days will be totally worth it.

» Dixie_Normous

Do you think he can go back next year for the handicapped running/ wheelchairing of the bulls?

FOR THOSE OF US IN THE NEWS BIZ, THERE IS ONLY ONE THING MORE EXCITING THAN HEAT.

Apparently I'm not the only one who has noticed that it gets hot in July.

Every year without fail, summer arrives. Also every year, sometime in late July, Mass Media goes collectively crazy for forty-eight hours and starts running Goddamn It's Hot Outside articles. I don't know who starts it, but once one media outlet runs It's Hot as its lead story, all the rest jump right in soon after. Using flashy TV lead-ins and 72-point fonts on front pages everywhere.

Why does July being hot rate such intense media coverage? Initially I thought it was due to staff meteorologists being a disgruntled bunch who hide out behind the sets of local TV news stations bitching and moaning to whoever will listen that they need more airtime because weather is important dammit. Finally, sometime around late July when everyone's worn down, the executive producer finally relents and lets the frustrated staff meteorologist have the lead story. This calms them down and keeps them content for another several months until the first huge snowstorm of the year hits.

I ran this by some media folks, and it turns out I was wrong. Mass Media always gives emphasis to the weather because it's a shared common experience. If it rains, we all get rained on. If it rains somewhere far away, we know what it's like to get rained on as well. One of my media friends said he worked in a local TV newsroom where the head guy had a mandate that weather would ALWAYS be the lead story unless something else was good enough to bump it from the top slot.

TV stations will do something similar in springtime when the first real storm system of the year hits. They'll give it wall-to-wall regular-program-interruption time the first time it happens. After that, they might put a live weather map in the bottom right corner of your screen. Maybe. And God forbid you live east of the city where the TV station is located, because local TV tends to stop coverage as soon as the storm leaves the metro area. This leaves all points east to wonder what the hell is going on and exactly where those tornadoes that local TV was tracking earlier got off to. Because the tornadoes didn't go away just because Mass Media stopped covering them.

This particular article was written by Tom Ferrick Jr., a columnist from *The Philadelphia Inquirer* who wondered aloud what in the hell the big deal was with heat in July. He notes that his newspaper sent out a team of reporters to scour the region, all of whom returned with reports that it was really hot outside, to the surprise of absolutely no one.

Counting overtime, the stations probably spent $250,000 yesterday to tell you that it is summer and that it is hot.

They had people standing in South Philadelphia, Center City, as far as Bucks County, and they reported back live that it was hot, everywhere.

Of course, they were wearing business suits and ties, so no wonder they were hot.

They should have followed some of the helpful hints we gave readers the other day about what to do when it gets hot.

Preach it, brother.

Ferrick also has another brilliant insight: Don't bother trying to buy an air-conditioner. "The managers of the stores tell us the air-conditioners are flying off the shelves. That's what they always say when we ask them. Of course, we never ask them until it is really hot."

Ferrick continues (I can't paraphrase this stuff any better than he says it):

For those of us in the news biz, there is only one thing more exciting than heat. It is record heat.

For record heat, we will remake the front page and use Pearl Harbor–sized type and write headlines that say: Record Heat Scorches Region!

We will then proceed to tell you that it was hot yesterday.

Television has us beat. It can tell you that it was hot today.

Ferrick deals with the question of sidebars, which are basically derivative articles of one main subject. In particular he notes that the Philly *Inquirer* sent reporters out into the region to find the stinkiest place due to the heat. They also planned to go out and ask people how they were coping with the heat. That's good for another article too. Ferrick says that by the time the media runs out of sidebars for how hot it is, it will be cold, and the process will start over.

It's refreshing to see that someone else out there in Mass Media land thinks this kind of thing is stupid too.

» Forbidden_Donut

Oh man, as a fellow journalist, I hear him on this one. It is news, but is it worth all the endless news resources we were all throwing at it?
/I'M REPORTING LIVE!!!

» Loabn

Record heat viciously murders family of five. What can you do to protect your family and keep heatmurderers out of your home? Is your daughter at risk of being heatraped? Is your son a heatqueer? More at 11.

» Addy2

Funny article. He needs to watch the Southern California news when it starts to sprinkle. The Storm Watch blasts on the local news beats the heat wave headlines for shear stupidity.

» Gals Panic

Does that guy even work for the news? He sounds like one of those, "Let the retired plummer write an op-ed column" kind of guys.

» Mr. Clarence Butterworth

It's not a true scorcher until some reporter tries to fry an egg on the sidewalk.

» Madcatcasey

If one more person says "It's a dry heat," I'm going to beat them in the face with an oar. I KNOW it's a dry heat. Everybody says it every year! Now STFU!

CDC WARNS THERE WILL BE A SHORTAGE OF FLU VACCINE THIS FALL, NOT UNLIKE LAST SIX YEARS.

This Seasonal Article is the most problematic, since it happens every single year and generally results in people dying. There's always a shortage of flu vaccine each year. The announcement comes just before the fall when people first start seeking inoculations.

Why does this happen every single year? That's not just a rhetorical question either; far as I'm concerned, there is no excuse for it. This particular year (2005), the problem was due to some sort of microbial contamination in the flu vaccine. The contamination rate was running roughly 3 percent. Obviously that's pretty unacceptable. The same thing happened in 2004, except the contamination came from a different factory in England. President Bush mentioned it in his State of the Union speech that year, much to the confusion of everyone because it was suddenly catapulted into the limelight as a major national crisis the following day only to be forgotten about completely thirty-six hours later. Obviously, because this crap keeps happening every year.

This Seasonal Article usually heralds the arrival of back-to-school season, the time of year when parents everywhere quiver at the thought of the vast number of bugs and viruses their children will soon bring home to spread to everyone else. A seasonal follow-up to this article comes usually in November or so when the CDC announces it has discovered that there is a strain of flu going around that the flu shot doesn't cover.

The article claims the problems inherent with contamination come from the fact that flu vaccine is made from fertilized chicken eggs. And we all know how clean chickens are. I'm surprised there hasn't been a bird flu Media Fearmongering crossover yet regarding the use of eggs in flu vaccine. I'm sure it will arrive eventually.

» Cager
And then once flu season is just about over, they will amazingly "discover" more vaccines they just happened to have laying around, but somehow completely forgot about.

» Tom_Thump
Very simple solution really. Just make up the balance with placebo shots, that stuff cures all kinds of shiat.

» Spoonfed'sBuddy
When will the pandemic hit and wipe out 3/4 of our population? I want West coast property before I get old . . . and I want it CHEAP!!!

ROLLING BLACKOUTS POSSIBLE IN CALIFORNIA TODAY. HELP CONSERVE ENERGY: TURN OFF YOUR AC AND TAKE OFF ALL YOUR CLOTHES.

Ah, crap. All right, forget what I said earlier; maybe this really is going to become an annual thing after all.

It turns out that San Francisco apparently doesn't have enough power capacity for everyone to turn on their air-conditioning all at the same time. While that does suck, apparently some of the blame lies in the lack of new power plants in California. Whether that is the fault of environmentalists or politicians is another story altogether.

So when temperatures hit 115 degrees for several days, the

state's power capacity was taxed to the limit. People were asked to turn off their air-conditioners, rolling blackouts ensued, cats and dogs living together, mass chaos. And then fall came and everyone forgot about it. Until next year.

» Pinatubo

I encourage all my fellow Californians to consume as much power as possible and promote the blackouts. I don't really feel like working today.

» C3

Dear Rolling Blackouts-

I would like you to stop by my office today at Universal Studios. I do not feel like working today and I would love to kick it with you. But please don't follow me home. Thank you.

» TheNewJesus

There was a time when no one had air conditioning. Be smart, you will survive, all of you.

» A Leaf in the Fall

Well . . . this makes me kind of happy that I live 15 miles from a Nuclear Power Plant. Haha, suckers!

» CavemanCometh

Canada thanks you for your power consumption. Please come again.

» Jument

People who live in an area that is prone to Problem X should not biatch about Problem X and should take appropriate personal precautions. And sometimes it is appropriate to move away when Problem X turns out to be more serious than originally anticipated. Such as living on the gulf coast below sea level or living on the coast of Florida. Your mileage may vary though. You can live anywhere you want but you can't (shouldn't?) get all whiney when one of your local hazards bites you in the ass.

2002: IT MUST BE FALL, TIME FOR THE YEARLY MEDIA DECLARATION THAT SATURDAY NIGHT LIVE ISN'T AS GOOD AS IT USED TO BE.

2003: TIME ONCE AGAIN FOR THE ANNUAL SATURDAY NIGHT LIVE SUCKS ARTICLES.

2004: SATURDAY NIGHT LIVE NEW SEASON BEGINS THIS WEEK, STILL UNFUNNY.

LOOKS LIKE WE ESCAPED LAST YEAR SOMEHOW, THOUGH.

Every fall, in late September or early October, Mass Media runs an article telling us that *Saturday Night Live* sucks. I remember seeing my first *Saturday Night Live* sucks article back in the late 1980s, wanting to vehemently disagree with the author. Nowadays I agree completely with them, but it's still a mystery as to why Mass Media feels compelled to remind us of this every year. It's as if *SNL* personally wronged them somehow and they're lashing out in revenge.

All of these articles have similar elements, including:

1. The show was sooooooo groundbreaking in the 1970s.

2. Reminding us that the best part of the show is Weekend Update.

3. Telling us that 1985 was the crappiest year ever for the show because Lorne Michaels wasn't there that year and the cast sucked.

4. The show has sucked since actor (insert flavor of the month here) left the show.

5. A happy fun ball reference.

6. Cast members regularly leave the show and later become successful, even though their movies are often steaming piles of poo.

7. And my favorite comment of all: "It was better ten years ago."

The "it was better ten years ago" comment is the best part, because it's a moving target, apparently. In the late 1980s and early 1990s, critics claimed that the show was well past its prime, much better ten years ago. Now those years are considered classics and today's shows are well past their prime. If anything, it's a testament to the show's consistent appeal to a specific age group. *SNL*'s humor level is a moving target. When you're younger, it's hilarious. When you get older, *SNL* sucks. Part of the attraction for the kids is staying up consistently that late for the first time. Being able to quote *SNL* bits to your twelve-year-old friends meant you had verbal proof you were up until 1:00 A.M., and that was some serious street cred right there. It probably doesn't hold true anymore, now that everyone watches *SNL* on DVR and YouTube instead of live.

In recent years, various authors of this annual article seem compelled to throw in an observation that Tina Fey is hot, which she is, and that *The Daily Show* is much funnier, which it is. Now that Tina Fey has left the show it remains to be seen if future articles will mention that she is hot. Maybe they will eventually idolize her as "the hottest cast member ever." It'll be another ten years before that happens, though. No word on when the "*Daily Show* was funnier ten years ago" articles are set to begin.

Mass Media also gave *SNL* a pass on this type of article in 2006, mainly because it was an almost entirely new cast and they probably thought *SNL* Sucks was implicit in the definition of "almost entirely new cast."

» **The Shoveler**

Even a blind hog finds the occasional acorn.

» **Confabulat**

Sure it's not that funny. And maybe it was funnier a long time ago.

But c'mon, was hearing "Cheeburger Cheeburger No Coke! Pepsi! Cheeburger Cheeburger" over and over again REALLY the comedy gold of the ages?

» **The_god_ninti**

Hey I say that year round.

» **StomachMonkey**

yeah I remember people talking about how it sucked back when Phil Hartman and Mike Meyers were on it. They'd go on and on about Dan Akroyd and John Belushi. Now those same people miss the "good old days" of Phil and Mike Meyers, even friggin Dana Carvey.

» **RockIsDead**

I liked it better when Johnny hosted it.

DEMOPOLIS NEWSPAPER ACKNOWL-EDGES PINS, NEEDLES, AND RAZORS IN HALLOWEEN GOODIES ARE BUNK, THEN TURNS AROUND AND ANNOUNCES FREE X-RAYING OF SAID HALLOWEEN GOODIES AT LOCAL HOSPITAL.

As I mentioned at the opening of this chapter, Seasonal Articles about poison and sharp objects in candy have morphed into articles about how this is all one huge urban legend. This article can't make up its mind which it wants to be, fearmonger or debunker, so now they cover both. First the article announces where you can get your candy X-rayed, then it goes on to discuss the urban legends surrounding finding scary stuff in candy. Then it goes one step further and highlights the fact that sometimes pins and things ARE found in candy but that kids' friends usually are the ones who put them in there. So wait, what the hell are they trying to say, exactly? That it's an urban legend but you should still panic anyhow?

The article recommends that parents inspect their kids candy before letting them eat it. Anyone who has gone trick-or-treating with kids knows this is pretty much impossible; they start stuffing it in their faces at the second or third house they visit. My parents used to look over our candy after trick-or-treating. They'd spread it out on the floor, sift through it a bit, grab a couple of pieces of something they wanted, and then declare it to be OK. I remember wondering how the hell they'd spot a tiny pinhole in the side of something with a wrapper on it, a wrapper that could have easily been removed and replaced. Now that I think about it, it's kind of similar to modern-day airport security.

Urban legends notwithstanding, who in the hell ever ate fruit they got while trick-or-treating? I remember getting the rare apple or box of raisins; those went right in the trash. No danger of accidentally finding poison or razors in those. If you really want to poison a kid, you better hide it in something they actually want to eat.

This article is pretty thorough in that it also manages to hit the other annual Halloween-related tips, such as put your kids in reflective clothing, give them a flashlight, and don't let little ones go out on their own. Just in case you didn't see this same crap last year or the year before or the year before that, going back to before you were even born.

Another staple of Halloween news articles is an interview with the Religious People Who Hate Fun who keep their kids inside from trick-or-treating and celebrate Jesusoween or whatever they call it. The people interviewed for these articles are probably under the impression that they're getting great publicity for their cause, not realizing that they're actually being laughed at by everyone.

As an aside, this particular Halloween there was one report of a guy who handed out poop duds instead of Milk Duds. I'm not sure if that's quite the same thing as finding sharp objects in candy.

Every Halloween we have a survey on Fark to ask what was the worst thing anyone ever got in their trick-or-treat stash as a kids. Winners have included bouillon cubes, ketchup packets, laxatives, expired coupons, pennies, and Taco Bell hot sauce.

» **Clold**

That's cool. It's not like there are lots of people without health insurance who could use some free xrays or anything.

» **Grumblecakes**

X-Rays don't detect PCP;)

» Clold

Based on my observations, a good 90–95% of children ages 5–10 produce high levels of PCP internally. My cousins kids are convinced they're super-human wrestleborgs. Gotta be the angel dust.

» Neonrisk

What a great idea! I am going to X-Ray my kids' food before every meal! I could X-Ray my kids' beds before bed-time! Maybe I'll Gamma-Ray their brains to make sure that the schools haven't been "corrupting the minds of the youth" again.

'TIS THE SEASON FOR FISTFIGHTS AT TOY STORES, FA LA LA LA LA, LA LA LA LA.

It turns out Black Friday, the day after Thanksgiving, is not the busiest shopping day of the year. That would actually be either Christmas Eve or the Sunday before Christmas, depending on what day Christmas falls on. If you think about it, it makes a certain amount of sense, because of course all the procrastinators would go shopping at the last possible moment all at the same time. And there are a hell of a lot of procrastinators.

The fact that Black Friday isn't real doesn't keep Mass Media from hyping it. Although more recently, just like with articles on Halloween candy, Mass Media is now both reporting on Black Friday and debunking it in the same article by telling us it was an urban legend. Gotta cover all the bases to appeal to morons and skeptics alike, not to mention the fact that it doubles the size of the article to be able to spend half the space talking about how fake something is.

Mass Media will usually run three articles on Black Friday.

Here Comes Black Friday articles start appearing during Thanksgiving week, definitely on Thanksgiving Day since the article can be written years in advance and run at the drop of a hat to fill space during a holiday when everyone is on vacation. Then on Black Friday itself there will be an article about how Today Is Black Friday, complete with interviews of local store managers and discussions of when they'll open, what's on sale, and estimates of how many shoppers they expect to have to Taser before noon. Then the following Monday it's the Black Friday recap, an article that tells whether retailers were pleased or discouraged by how much crap people bought over the weekend. This one is pretty much just culled from various press releases from the big box stores.

One of the other articles you'll usually see is whether any Black Friday fights occurred, and if they did, where it happened. These articles appeal to everyone's inner wrestling fan. We love the thought of 300-pound blue hairs squaring off over a sale on toaster ovens. It's compelling stuff, and complete garbage, but we get it every year anyhow. Usually someone ends up in the hospital.

Has anyone else noticed that all these "bargain hunters" just sell all this marked-down Black Friday merchandise on eBay? Are there any Real Black Friday Shoppers anymore?

» Scape

   Capitalism at it's finest. God bless this country.

» Oldfarthenry

   Another article from the same source:
      Nasal Spray Arouses Women's Desire To Have Sex In Minutes.
      Dammit, post this as a newsflash!

» Kev1976

   I hate how the media continues to say today is the busiest shopping day of
   the year. Then the day after Christmas, they say that is the busiest day of the

year. I guess they are banking on the very short term memories of their viewers.

» Fleener

As I rained blows upon him, I realized there had to be another way!

» Honeytrap

It seems like every year Wal-Mart runs some insane Black Friday sale with shock prices that culminates with shoppers being stomped and/or law enforcement involvement. Were I conspiracy-minded, I would think they did this just for the sake of causing some mini-riot in order to make the news.

Hey! Free publicity!

» Inflatable Jesus

I was going to go shopping today, but then I decided it would be more fun to lay out my scrotum on the cutting board and pound my testicles flat with the meat mallet, then saw my weener off with the serrated bread knife, feed it to the dog, pour vinegar in the hole where my dick used to be, bathe myself in vodka, set myself on fire, and rest my hands on hot stove burners while repeatedly banging my head on the edge of the stove.

When I started to pick up the meat mallet, though, I realized I didn't have to do either.

/makes note to put cutting board in the dishwasher.

CYBER MONDAY, THE TRADITIONAL BUSIEST DAY OF THE YEAR FOR ONLINE SHOPPING. EXCEPT IT IS ACTUALLY THE TWELFTH BUSIEST AND THE TERM WAS INVENTED SOMETIME LAST WEEK.

From the moment the term *Cyber Monday* appeared in Mass Media, it was patently obvious that someone just made this horseshit up. And what do you want to bet we're stuck with the term *Cyber Monday* from now until the Internet collapses or becomes self-aware and kills us all? At the very least Mass Media will likely continue to run Seasonal Articles about how Cyber Monday isn't real, even though no one believed it in the first place. Because, just like with Black Friday, debunking it doubles the size of the article, giving Cyber Monday twice the space-occupying power of the original version.

This term popped up for the first time in 2005, plucked straight out of a successful Unpaid Placement Masquerading as Actual Article from the National Retail Federation. They claimed that online stores saw a huge rise in sales the Monday after the Friday after Thanksgiving. Online stores were quick to point out that actual online sales are pretty much spread across December 5–15, again depending on what day Christmas actually falls. According to Wikipedia, meaning this crap could be completely made up but probably isn't, the busiest online shopping day in 2005 was December 12.

Mass Media didn't care that it was almost completely fabricated, however. They seized on the opportunity to have another three articles worth of filler to be able to roll out the door during the Thanksgiving holiday period. Between these articles, Black Monday articles, and regular ads, newspapers likely were able to fill up six full pages in their entirety with this crap, minimum. That's assuming they didn't split each article across two pages, which they probably did. Twelve pages is almost an entire news-paper section in itself.

As a testament to how effectively Mass Media can spread complete and utter garbage, the day after Cyber Monday, if you typed the term into Google it returned 779,000 results. That's a little less than half the number of results you get if you type in the term "quantum physics."

The numbers of results the same search returned at the time of this writing was significantly lower, but just wait until next year.

» Mugato

Don't let something like the facts ruin a perfectly marketable media buzz-word.

» Lord of Allusions

As soon as I heard that on the news, I sarcastically thought, "That had to have been made up last week."

» Most Delicious Worm

On Cyber Monday I bought porn subscriptions for all my loved ones.
    Except my cousin Amber, who's already got her own line of videos.

» Cyberlost

You mean to tell me that the media tried to influence me to buy something?

» SwankyWanky

This year people will be able to buy gifts over the internet, or "on line" as technology buffs like to call it.

» Freshly Baked Muffin

What happened to the days when it was just "the day after Thanksgiving" or "Christmas Eve" or "Shit, its Monday, time to go back to work."

» Ixtacoyotl

Why didn't any of the news agencies inform me about "Super Coca Cola Tuesday"!!! I'm so glad you let me know, otherwise I would have heard about it on TONIGHT'S news and it would have been too late

» Braedan

Cyber Monday?

    bloodninja: Baby, I been havin a tough night so treat me nice aight?
    BritneySpears14: Aight.
    bloodninja: Slip out of those pants baby, yeah.
    BritneySpears14: I slip out of my pants, just for you, bloodninja.
    bloodninja: Oh yeah, aight. Aight, I put on my robe and wizard hat.
    BritneySpears14: Oh, I like to play dress up.
    bloodninja: Me too baby.
    BritneySpears14: I kiss you softly on your chest.
    bloodninja: I cast Lvl. 3 Eroticism. You turn into a real beautiful woman.

BritneySpears14: Hey . . .

bloodninja: I meditate to regain my mana, before casting Lvl. 8 chicken of
  the Infinite.

BritneySpears14: Funny I still don't see it.

» Popinjay

In other news, Blowjob Friday is coming up this week.

COST OF TWELVE DAYS OF CHRISTMAS WENT UP 6.1 PERCENT OVER LAST YEAR. AVIAN FLU TO BLAME.

One of the more ingenious (or insidious) Seasonal Marketing-Related Not News Articles is the Cost of the Twelve Days of Christmas article. Every year the fine folks at PNC Advisors release a cost analysis of all the gifts given in the popular Christmas song, and every year Mass Media just runs the damn thing verbatim without giving it a second thought.

We see this article every year for the same reasons we see Black Friday articles every year: It's prewritten and can be thrown into the news hopper over the holiday break.

PNC Advisors is nice enough to break down the costs of all of the items, including the percentage gain or loss compared to last year. Then they invent explanations for the changes in price, such as oil prices or, in this case, avian flu restricting the shipment of birds internationally. EVERYBODY PANIC. PNC Advisors has also started including a different listing for what it would cost to buy on the Internet as opposed to shopping traditionally. This of course takes up even more space.

And speaking of waste of space, this article certainly qualifies. The subject can't possibly have any relevance to anyone's daily life. Unless you're an exotic bird farmer in Asia, that is.

» Eraser8

I don't think I've ever really paid attention to the number of bird-related gifts in that list.

Strange.

» Popstop

How the hell do you calculate lords a-leaping?

» Ookdalibrarian

Go to the local pub, calculate how much you need to spend to get one average customer "as drunk as a lord" and multiply by ten.

I should note it doesn't cost anything to get a drunk to "leap," being drunk, they'll gladly jump anything, usually to the cry of "hey, fellas, watch this!!!"

YEAR-END WRAP-UP

The basic form: Top 10 Stories of the Year.

The advanced form to allow for more articles to kill more space: The Top 10 Most (relevant/popular) (news/sports/entertainment/science/weird) Stories of the (year/decade/century).

There are way too many examples to choose just one of these articles. Every single Mass Media outlet runs at least one, if not several, versions of this story.

It used to be these articles would appear during the holiday period between Christmas and New Year's Day. However, in recent times it seems there is some sort of race among Mass Media outlets to be the first to establish what the Top 10 Stories of the Year actually are. Each Mass Media outlet has a different idea of what the top ten are, after all.

As a result, the release dates of these articles keeps backing up. It's getting to the point where the Best of the Year articles are skipping December entirely. In 2006, for example, some idiot Mass

Media outfit released a Top 10 Advertisements of the Year in freakin' August. That's sure as hell jumping the gun. I remember seeing Best of the Decade lists in 1998. I also remember a Best of the Millennium article running in the late 1980s. Best Innovation: The Fork. Personally I would have gone with indoor plumbing.

Things get really embarrassing when Mass Media outlets release the Top 10 Most Popular Stories based solely on Web site traffic. The first media outfit I remember seeing do this was a North Carolina newspaper. They prefaced the article with a long disclaimer about how the list was based solely on traffic and that no one should under any circumstances write to complain about the content of the list because they sure as hell didn't pick it. I don't remember exactly how many of the top ten had to do with sex; it was either all of them or nine of them. I'm hedging because it's certainly possible that one of the ten wasn't about sex, but based on my personal experience watching outbound traffic patterns on Fark, I doubt it. The top story of the year based solely on Web traffic: man caught having sex with his dog.

Nowadays, Mass Media has no qualms whatsoever about hiding behind the flimsy argument that popular news items are somehow important or relevant. Witness the train wrecks that are the Most Popular News section of any Mass Media outlet. Conclusion: People sure do like sex a lot. Well, duh. How about telling me something I don't know? Surely there's a war on somewhere.

Happy New Year.

Media Fatigue

MASS MEDIA TRIES TO DO A SIMPLE JOB. STEP 1: FIND THE NEWS. Step 2: Report it. In theory that should be all there is to it. In practice, this is not the case. Sometimes news stories get completely out of control and take on a life of their own. This is usually never good. It's as if Mass Media gets so excited about an event that they can't bring themselves to stop reporting about it, even long after there's any reason to continue talking about it. You would think this would happen only with important stories, but no.

Mass Media can really run an article on a story only once unless something changes. Take popular humorous news Web sites, for example. Mass Media can write an initial article about them, something to the effect of "Check out this new popular humorous news site." Once that's done, they can't run a story about the Web site again, because nothing has changed. Occasionally they can get away with running a similar story years later by passing it off as retro analysis. "That guy running that still-popular humorous Web site has been at it for ten years now." In order to write another story, something has to change. For example, the author of the site could write a book. Now it's possible to interview him again. There's a concept for you.

Mitigating factors are one of several reasons the media could run your story again. Here's my favorite example: Norwegian environmental group Fuck for Forest is famous (in Norway at least) for doing media stunts to draw attention to environmental issues. At a concert by the death metal band Cumshots, the two members of Fuck for Forest started having sex on stage. Amazingly, this behavior is illegal in Norway. The couple was promptly arrested. This made the media rounds for about a day, then dropped off the radar. Two weeks later, while being arraigned, the male member of Fuck for Forest answered the judge's question "How do you plead?" by dropping trou. Back into the media it went again.

That was atypical for your average crime story. Crime generally warrants at least one and as many as three media mentions per incident during their media life cycle.

The first media mention comes right after the actual event, the second media mention occurs when the trial begins, and the third comes at sentencing. In the process of writing successive articles on the same subjects, journalists will go back to their original article, copy and paste most or all of the previous article, and add any new events relating to the subject matter at the top. Sometimes they'll reword the previous articles when they recycle them, sometimes not.

For example, let's say you shoot your buddy Earl accidentally. The first article out of the gate will pretty much be exactly that: Dumbass Accidentally Shoots Friend.

The second article about the event will roll out the door when your trial comes up. Dumbass Who Accidentally Shot Friend Goes to Trial. The first paragraph of the new article will say you went to trial to be charged with manslaughter. The whole rest of the article will be copied and pasted, with perhaps a few subtle changes and/or additions of minor things that have happened since the accident, such as how you cried like a girl when asked for comment or how Earl's family tried to have you put away for life. How much beer you were drinking at the time usually gets mentioned as well, because that's "bad." The media will tack those kinds of details on wherever, assuming they can find them.

The third article comes out when the sentence is handed down. Dumbass Receives (0–1000) Years in Prison for Shooting Friend. Again, the news information, in this case the prison sentence, will be the first paragraph, followed by yet another copy and paste of the original article. This allows the journalist writing the article to turn in an entire piece after about fifteen minutes of so-called work, giving him ample time to finish off that day's sudoku puzzle or surf more tentacle porn than usual from his work computer.

Every single mitigating factor is an excuse to write one more article by producing a paragraph of actual new material, pasting on the previous story, and calling this a new article. Bearing this in mind, consider what happens when mitigating factors continue to roll in fast and furious with no end in sight. Mass Media loses all modicum of self-control. They can't stop themselves.

Out-of-control media stories can be further compounded by what Mass Media calls "sidebars." As mentioned in the previous chapter on Seasonal Articles, sidebars are related stories, but with slightly different subject matter. For example, let's say the headline of the day is It's Damn Hot Outside. A sidebar article would be the inevitable frying-an-egg-on-the-sidewalk trick. Or asking people about how hot they think it is. Every man-on-the-street interview you've ever seen is a sidebar. Sidebar stories can't exist without the main story to support them.

Non-crime stories that receive more than one filed report are an entirely different beast. Most commonly, this formula is reserved for breaking news. Unfortunately sometimes what Mass Media thinks fits the mold of breaking news isn't really news.

ANATOMY OF MEDIA FATIGUE

Step 1: News Breaks

Step 2: Issue Retractions

Step 3: Talk It to Death

Step 4: Can't... Stop... Talking...

Step 5: Has the Media Gone Too Far?

Step 1: News Breaks

An incident occurs, Mass Media kicks into high gear. News anchors ad-lib like crazy, news Web sites release constant updates. Everyone is in full media blather mode. Sometimes during a breaking news event, Mass Media runs out of stuff to talk about while waiting for the ongoing event itself to end. Witness the debacle of the 2000 U.S. presidential election. Forty-eight hours passed before most news networks finally and reluctantly decided to halt nonstop coverage. Dan Rather was so far off the rails that he was interviewing parking garage attendants by the forty-seventh hour, trying desperately to stay awake after two nights with no sleep.

During breaking news events, you'll often see Mysterious Repeating Sources. Here's a priceless example.

Dimebag Darrell was the former lead guitarist for Pantera. After playing with Pantera for years he decided to leave and work on some new projects, one of which included a new band, Damageplan.

In December 2004, Nathan Gale, a fan of Pantera who blamed Dimebag for their breakup, showed up at a Damageplan concert with a loaded 9mm handgun. He jumped up on stage and shot Dimebag Darrell in the head three times. He fired several other shots, managing to kill three other people before a security guard returned fire with a shotgun and killed the crazed fan. As an aside, it was discovered after the fact that Gale's handgun had thirty-five bullets left in it. Things could certainly have been worse.

The morning after the shooting occurred, I was sitting in on a morning show for WXZZ 103.3 FM in Lexington, Kentucky, a classic/modern rock station. People called in all morning asking for more details, but since it had happened just hours before, there wasn't much information. At the time no one knew who had been killed, how many people had been killed, or pretty much any other details about it.

I started combing wire reports and other news sites to try to find out what had happened. I was able to find multiple mentions of a witness claiming that one of the band's members, Vinnie, used his cell phone to call someone right after the shooting. Listeners were interested in that bit of information, so I started tracking it to see where it had come from. Turns out it had been mentioned once on a Pantera message board far, far down the comment thread. Yet every media outlet was repeating it.

What are the odds that every Mass Media outlet had read that same message board? Zero. How did this tidbit end up on every Mass Media outlet? They heard it on the news. From each other. And from Fark, where it turns out this bit of information originated.

One Fark reader, a Pantera fan, had seen the discussion on the board and posted a link to it on Fark. NBC4i.com picked up the link and ran with it on their news coverage. Within the hour, every mainstream news source had tacked that detail onto its news coverage. Did Vinnie really use someone's cell phone right after the shooting? I have no idea. It was on a message board on the Internet, something you would not usually consider a reliable source. Yet this detail was reported on every newscast about the incident.

Mysterious Repeating Sources are caused by the fact that news sources do a minimum amount of background research, especially during breaking news. If a piece of information originates with research they themselves did, they tend to do a decent job of fact-checking it before reporting it. If it originates with someone else, Mass Media, or other blog-type media, they tend not to fact-check it at all. It's well known that all Mass Media sources keep an eye on one another. Every major TV network has a main control room where you will find any number of TVs tuned to any number of different news sources you can imagine. I suspect this is at least part of the reason they jump down each other's throats over bad research, plagiarism, and the like. Inaccurate Mysterious Repeating Sources make everyone look stupid, even though the real culprit is copycatting and bad fact-checking.

Several people working at various news outlets have told me that at one time or another, their respective news organization has run a breaking news story solely because the competition ran the story first. This would be as opposed to running a breaking news story because they had firsthand concrete information. The news anchor is notified of breaking news and has to announce it without any information whatsoever other than "something" has "happened." The networks then scramble to gather news while the anchor stalls for time. Oftentimes, the initial breaking news article is cobbled together entirely from other news sources with no background checks.

The absolute worst-case scenario is when a wire service gets something wrong. As far as I can tell, no news outlet ever hesitates to post anything that appears on the AP or Reuters. One example of this was an article the AP ran that turned out to be an urban legend. It concerned a woman getting stuck in a suction toilet on a transatlantic flight—perhaps you heard about this one. A woman flushes a suction toilet while sitting on it and becomes stuck, having to spend the rest of the flight on the can until a rescue crew can pry her loose. Most versions of this story (which turned out to be an urban myth) include the detail that the woman is fat, which apparently makes it funnier.

Mysterious Repeating Sources abounded on 9/11/2001. The media reported some pretty large inaccuracies, such as: a Palestinian group claiming responsibility by 9:40 A.M.; a car bomb near the Pentagon; a helicopter bomb near the Pentagon; the National Mall was on fire; a second explosion in DC; the south wall of the White House was on fire; a second plane was being tracked as heading toward the Pentagon; there were sixteen missing flights still in the air as of 10:30 A.M.; 35,000–50,000 casualties; and so on. The list goes on and on but you get the idea. Reporting news during breaking events is difficult, there is no doubt about that. But exactly how did every news organization end up reporting all of these claims as fact?

They copied them from each other and assumed the original source had checked them out. Yes, I realize they probably said the words "sources tell us" before most of these "facts," but let's be serious, no one hears that being said. That just keeps Mass Media from being liable if the information is wrong.

Step 2: Issue Retractions

Usually a day after the incident occurs, the media rolls out a series of retractions and corrections. In their haste to be the first to report on breaking news, Mass Media inadvertently passes on a number of inaccurate details. When breaking news hits, usually the only available information is from stunned witnesses, many of whom probably can't accurately remember what it was they witnessed. Police aren't much good as sources of information either; they're prohibited from making statements that haven't been proven in court. This is why you often see them talking around their actual theories with a series of true statements. "Yes, the man was found with eight gallons of Vaseline. Yes, the walls and floors were covered with it. Yes, he was watching a pornographic movie. Was there a sex act involved? No comment (wink-wink)."

Step 3: Talk It to Death

After the media retractions comes the analysis. Mass Media trots out all the talking heads and the special experts. They write entire articles and produce entire shows that consist solely of opinion-based diatribes. Oftentimes Mass Media will punch them up for shock value, especially when dealing with politics.

Step 4: Can't . . . Stop . . . Talking . . .

Having used up all the real news, Mass Media starts reporting on sidebar incidents. My favorite example is a Seasonal Article: shark attacks. Mass Media usually doesn't get going on shark attacks until the first person is mauled by one. Then every other day there will be an article about shark sightings, shark tour boats, shark habits, sharks aren't really that dangerous, hey, what's Steven Spielberg up to these days, and more shark attacks. Sharks don't really attack people all that often, but once the media gets going on a subject, it just can't stop itself. There were only two groups of people happy about 9/11 (other than the perpetrators). One was sharks. The other was Gary Condit. Remember him? Probably not. He was a congressman who was never accused of but heavily suspected of killing an intern. He was front page news right up until September 10. Come to think of it, he was probably front page news the morning of the eleventh, but after that he faded away, never to be seen again.

When Mass Media runs out of sidebar articles to discuss, they start reaching. This results in articles on incidents that are only vaguely related to the initial event. During the first launch of the space shuttle after the *Columbia* disaster, Mass Media started writing articles based on complete fiction: What if the space shuttle has to land in California instead of Florida, and what if it overshoots and hits L.A.? How much damage would there be? That was an actual article.

Step 5: Has the Media Gone Too Far?

This is the end of the media cycle and the beginning of true Media Fatigue. Has the Media Gone Too Far is to breaking news as a caboose is to a train. Mass Media starts to suspect, probably via e-mails and phone calls complaining about too much coverage, that they've Gone Too Far. They then decide that that topic makes a good subject for a story. Sometimes this phase actually goes on too long, going as far as having the media break out the talking heads to discuss whether there's been too much media coverage. In excessive cases they'll run Has the Media Gone Too Far for several days, perhaps even repeatedly.

CHENEY'S GOT A GUN. DAYS IN MASS MEDIA: 8

On February 11, 2006, Vice President Cheney and an entourage of fellow hunters and Secret Service agents were out hunting quail on a Texas ranch. At some point, Cheney lost track of Harry Whittington (a lobbyist friend) and accidentally shot him. Whittington was struck in the chest and head and rushed to the hospital. Sounds pretty straightforward, doesn't it?

Mass Media would have none of that.

There's no doubt in my mind that it was an accident. Had Whittington been a protestor or, say, Al Franken, there would be room for some suspicion. An accidental shooting is an unfortunate incident that can happen to anyone on a hunting trip. In fact, soon after the Cheney incident, a man on a hunting trip accidentally shot his friend while making a joke about Cheney accidentally shooting a man on a hunting trip. That follow-up incident generated only one round of media attention. Cheney, being vice president of the United States, garnered significantly more media attention. Some would say (that would be me) too much attention.

Unfortunately, Cheney Accidentally Shoots Friend happened during a slow news week. It also happened at the beginning of the week as opposed to Friday, when around noontime all news-gathering activities grind to a halt for the weekend. It was also a slow news week in a slow news month. Involving a vice president of an administration that had yet to answer some questions about some doings regarding blowing up countries or something. An administration that regularly punished members of the media for asking harsh questions by sending them to the back of the room during press conferences. The media was ready to rip someone a new one, and they had a bunch of column inches that needed filling. Cheney gave them a perfect target.

The news of the shooting hit the wires on the afternoon of February 12, the day after the accident. I was out drinking or taking a nap or something at the time (NFL season was over),

and apparently so were the other Fark admins, because it didn't
get posted to Fark for several hours. This resulted in the Farkers
holding their own contest to see who could submit the most
amusing Cheney shooting tagline. This happens during any news
flash–level event that doesn't get posted for a while, partly out of
boredom and partly out of frustration that people keep submit-
ting the links to Fark nonstop until we put it to the main page. If
it weren't for the timeliness issue, it would almost be worth it to
not post any breaking news for a few hours just to give them time
to come up with a much funnier headline.

Among those submitted:

CHENEY BEGINS COUP

DICK CHENEY, IN A DESPERATE BID TO REAFFIRM THE GOP'S
NATIONAL SECURITY CREDENTIALS, CAPS A BITCH

DICK CHENEY, FED UP WITH HOSPITAL WAITING LISTS, DECIDES TO
BEGIN HARVESTING ORGANS ON HIS OWN

CHENEY TAKES TORT REFORM ONE STEP TOO FAR

DICK CHENEY INJURES FRIEND IN EXTREME BUKAKE INCIDENT

Unless you've got a photographic memory or for some reason
remember this story as clear as day (if so, seek help), you probably
missed the first mitigating factor guaranteed to give the story
another go-around in the press: The news hit the wires the day
after the accident. The vice president of the United States shoots
someone in the head and chest and no one finds out about it till
the following day. *Editor & Publisher* did a bit of sleuthing to find
out how this happened; turns out the only reason it was that
SOON was the owner of the land called a buddy of hers over at
the *Corpus Christi Caller-Times* to let him know. The reporter called

Cheney's office for confirmation; they gave it. The article was written, and the media firestorm ensued.

When Cheney spokesman Lea Anne McBride was asked if they ever planned to inform the media had the media not contacted them, she refused comment. Well, duh. The implication here is that Cheney's office never intended to contact the media. As if they planned to cover it all up and go on as if nothing happened. Despite the fact that it was arguably an M.O. of the Bush administration to cover things up, there's no way in hell they planned to attempt it in this case. In the event that they tried to cover it up, how long would it be before the press eventually found out and a true media shitstorm erupted? McBride just wasn't willing to walk into that trap. McBride wouldn't have commented if the media had asked if Dick Cheney had ever blown a goat either. That no doubt would have resulted in media coverage to the effect of "When asked if Dick Cheney had ever blown a goat, his spokesperson refused comment rather than deny it." She refused comment because it was a leading question. It's much more likely that Cheney's office just bungled the whole thing. Now that I think about it, I'm not sure that's more reassuring.

Editor & Publisher went on to say that at a Monday press conference *The New York Times* observed that Press Secretary Scott McClellan couldn't answer any questions on the matter. He didn't know when President Bush learned about it. He didn't know Cheney had shot anyone until Sunday. It's odd that *The New York Times* mentions press corps irritation given that absolutely no one in the press corps thinks the press secretary knows shit about anything. That's his whole job: to not know shit about anything. He is specifically kept out of important meetings for the sole purpose of his not being able to accidentally say something he shouldn't. He has no idea what the hell is going on. And the media knows it. They just like badgering the guy.

The whole point of having a press conference with a press secretary who knows nothing really makes no sense at all. And it's not like President Bush invented this process. Clinton's press secretary didn't know anything either. Neither did his Republican predecessor. The media is well aware of this fact, which begs the question, Why do they even bother to show up and ask questions? Answer: It takes up space in media. Without news you can't sell ads. Expect the media to continue to react with indignation in the future when lo and behold, the current press secretary is completely out of the loop.

All joking aside, it is a valid question. Why did it take so long for news of this to reach the media? Numerous involved parties were asked, from the administration to the hospital to the landowner to the local sheriff's department. They all gave different excuses, none of them really any good.

The truth probably lies somewhere along these lines: Had Cheney been shot by Whittington, would the same reporting delay have happened? Doubtful; there are protocols for when something of that nature occurs. Administrations and media know what to do when a major government official is killed during term. In fact since 1840 it has happened about every twenty years or so to a sitting president.

The reverse, where a sitting member of an administration shot someone else, hadn't happened in over two hundred years. Then Vice President Aaron Burr shot and killed Alexander Hamilton in a duel, resulting in Hamilton's visage on the $20 bill and Aaron Burr getting an annoying prickly weed named after him (as far as I know). No one remembers who Burr was, and few people know that Hamilton is one of two "non-presidents on a denomination of U.S. currency that *hasn't* failed horribly who most people could not name if their lives depended on it." (Ben Franklin is the other, but everyone knows who he is thanks to that kite thing, a fact he'd probably be somewhat pissed off about if he were alive, considering all his other accomplishments.)

The Burr–Hamilton duel happened well before the modern media was established. Odds are the handling of the Cheney shooting was just botched due to lack of protocol. But that answer won't sell papers. The previously antagonized and irritated media painted it to look like some possible administration conspiracy to keep them in the dark. Many stories insinuated that perhaps this lack of information was some kind of pattern that related to other issues, such as Weapons of Mass Destruction, Invading Iraq, 9/11, Halliburton, Jimmy Hoffa, and so on. I'm not saying Cheney isn't a jackass, I'm just saying his staff probably really truly screwed the pooch on this one.

Further articles about this side issue can be summed up as follows:

MEDIA TO CHENEY'S OFFICE: You guys fucked up.

CHENEY'S OFFICE: Nuh-UH (provides revisionist evidence).

MEDIA: Did too (disputes revisionist evidence).

CHENEY'S OFFICE: Did not (provides additional revisionist evidence).

And so on. Seriously, this crap went on for a week.

The media couldn't have run any more new articles about the situation without new information. On Monday, February 13, they got some. It was announced that Cheney, cheap-ass bastard, hadn't paid for a $7 stamp to shoot upland game birds on the infamous trip. The horror. The media ran this one up the flagpole and got some traction on it from people who didn't actually read the arti- cle. Cheney and Whittington did each have a $125 hunting license, but neither had a $7 stamp to shoot upland game birds. Cheney's staff got the blame for this one, and they passed the buck, saying they asked but no one told them about it. No harm, no foul.

The next mitigating factor allowing the media to go around the bend one more time on this story was that on Tuesday, that poor bastard Whittington ended up having a heart attack in the hospital. Out came the word processors, two paragraphs of surgical descriptions were written, one quick copy and paste of yesterday's news, and *BLAM!* Time for a smoke break. For the rest of the day, see you at the bar.

For the next mitigating factor, a true scandal was revealed: Cheney said he had had "one beer." Oh. My. God. Stop the presses. Never mind the fact that beer is pretty much the only point to hunting. If you've never been hunting, it's just like fishing. If you've never been fishing, it's just like golf. If you've never been golfing, these activities have two things in common: They're really, really boring and half the point is to drink constantly while doing it.

I seriously doubt that Cheney had just one beer. Ask any police officer what they hear when they pull someone over for driving erratically. "Have you been drinking tonight, sir?" "Yes, officer, just one beer." Then the driver promptly blows a BAC high enough that the officer gets a contact high from the vapor and can't legally drive now either.

The media would have people believe that high school kids, college kids, and politicians don't touch a drop of alcohol. It's certainly not the case. If you ever want to see some drunk-ass politicians, stop by the Frankfort Holiday Inn in the evening sometime with the Kentucky State Legislature is in session. It reminds me of the old Looney Tunes cartoons about Sam Sheepdog and Ralph Wolf, where they go to work every morning chatting about random stuff, but once they clock in, it's on. They fight all morning, take a lunch break together, fight all afternoon. That's government, folks. The Cheney beer issue allowed a little righteous indignation to creep into the mix.

Cheney ended up holding a press conference on Wednesday, February 15. With so much time to fill before the press conference (at the time, no one actually knew if and when it would be held) and no new information forthcoming, and with the media knowing that eventually there would be a follow-up press conference or something (or an interview with a sympathetic media outlet), they had to write some more crap to fill empty space.

It wasn't so much of a mitigating factor as it was a sort of side effect, but for those three days between announcement and press conference, any poor asshole who shot anyone accidentally made the front page of every Web site in the country. I already mentioned the unfortunate bastard who accidentally shot his friend after joking about Cheney doing the same thing; that got an extra dose of attention (speaking of mitigating factors). Another incident involved a shooting where the shooter actually claimed he mistook his friend's elbow for a squirrel.

At this point the media was out of mitigating factors, and Cheney didn't announce he was giving a press conference until Wednesday. Now that there was a serious shortage of new material, it was time to run some sidebars.

Everyone's favorite media whore organization, PETA, decided to pipe up for some Unpaid Placement Masquerading as Actual Article and issue a denunciation of Cheney hunting animals. "I hope that the man you mistook for a quail is doing well," said PETA spokesman Who Gives a Rat's Ass. "Put down your guns and pick up a tennis racket," they encouraged. Copy, paste, smoke break, bar, beer. Out for the rest of the day.

James and Sarah Brady popped up from wherever they've

been to issue a press release as well. I'll just plunk it down here; if Mass Media can do it, I can too:

WASHINGTON, Feb. 12/U.S. Newswire/—James and Sarah Brady made comments today related to Vice President Cheney's reportedly accidental shooting yesterday in Texas.

"Now I understand why Dick Cheney keeps asking me to go hunting with him," said Jim Brady. "I had a friend once who accidentally shot pellets into his dog—and I thought he was an idiot."

"I've thought Cheney was scary for a long time," Sarah Brady said. "Now I know I was right to be nervous."

What. The. Hell? Your feelings about James and Sarah Brady aside, that's a press release? That's seriously the entire thing. Even scarier, it got picked up in some news outlets as an honest-to-god article.

Out came the talking heads, who we can't really pin the blame on for this one, since they talk only when asked. Dallas defense attorney David Finn, who the article mentions had also been a prosecutor, in case that means something to you (oh, wow, he's, like, twice a lawyer, he must know what he's talking about), said that a Texas grand jury could bring a charge of negligent homicide if there was evidence that Cheney "knew or should have known there was a substantial or unjustifiable risk that his actions would result in him shooting a fellow hunter." He could face up to two years in jail if convicted. Holy Veeps in Jail, Batman!

But oh, wait, never mind. Later on in the article it says prosecutors did not have an investigation under way. They followed up that tidbit with a quote from the poor bastard who would have had to prosecute the case: "If something unfortunate happens, then we'll decide what to do, then we'll decide whether we're going to have an investigation or not." What the hell does that mean? I don't think he was being cagey, I think he was a deer in the media headlights who just blurted out the first sentence he could string together to get them to go away. As far as the media is concerned, when quoting directly, the less sense the quote makes and more embarrassing it is, the better. If it's really bad they might get an extra article out of the deal.

In the kind of twist that happens only when an event is somewhat amusing, instead of reporting on the media, an article appeared reporting on what comedians were saying. Fark.com got a few write-ups on this one. It was a collection of late-night host quotes, blog postings, etc. You'll occasionally see this type of article appear if (1) the situation is funny in some way and (2) if the situation is still ongoing. The latter is more important, because the media can't wrap it all up with Has the Media Gone Too Far until everything's said and done. By the time this article came out, they were still trying to find funny quotes. That's almost as good as not working.... Hey, wait a minute.

So Cheney didn't get around to holding a press conference on the matter until February 15. I can't say that I blame him. If I'd shot a guy accidentally and knew I'd get asked by the media if I had sex with a goat, I wouldn't have been too eager to call a press conference either. He took the easy way out by going on Fox News and having some softball questions tossed at him, which in all honesty was probably fine. People with an ax to grind against him or his administration (ha-ha) were disappointed with this, but let's be real, what could they have possibly discovered if he had been up in front of a room of disgruntled journalists angry at their treatment over other unrelated Bush Administration issues?

After the press conference, someone from the AP went to talk to Christus Spohn Hospital administrator Peter Banko, who said Whittington was mystified by all the attention over the incident.

That's a damn good question. What was the point of all this? What else was there to discover in all this? Other than embarrass his office staffers for bungling the media relations on an event that hadn't happened in two hundred years, nothing really. It wasn't like he was going to break down after some serious questioning and admit he knew all along that Iraq had nothing to do with 9/11. And you can bet your ass someone would have asked that.

When Whittington finally got out of the hospital a week later, he apologized for getting shot. Which immediately cleared up all controversy on the issue and satisfied everyone. Also that same day, Has the Media Gone Too Far articles started showing up, signaling the end of the news cycle, just in time. Until this rehashing of the events.

JACKSON MEDIA MALFUNCTION

During the halftime show for Super Bowl XXXVIII, Janet Jackson's right nipple made an unexpected appearance. Hilarity ensued.

I didn't actually see it happen. I was at a Fark party during Super Bowl XXXVIII at the Hooters Casino in a small town next to Vegas. During halftime I decided to go play some blackjack because I was having an incredible string of luck that trip. I played twenty minutes, won a couple hundred dollars, and went back to the Hooters restaurant where we had been watching the game. Perhaps it was the dozen or so beers I'd consumed during the first half, but I don't recall people talking about the halftime show in the bar there. Hooters had also put on a wings contest at halftime where they served the contestants wings doused in battery acid or something, so perhaps no one else in the bar saw it either.

Later I discovered that people who did actually see it didn't realize what it was they had seen until later. In fact there were more than a few media articles whose authors said when they saw it, they couldn't confirm it. So they went to Fark to find out, figuring we'd probably have something up about it first. Turns out they made the right call. One of the admins, HPZ, was watching the Super Bowl and, unlike me, was near his computer at the time. He posted the first screen cap submitted to Fark, which incidentally appeared under a minute after the incident. Farkers are damn fast with this kind of thing. HPZ then spent the rest of the evening redirecting traffic to other submitted screen caps because the crush of traffic from people wanting to see Janet Jackson's boob was so huge we were literally wiping out site after site like some giant Internet magnifying glass picking off Internet ants one by one.

Not surprisingly, Mass Media didn't have anything to say about it until Monday. This is due at least in part to the fact that media folks aren't really excited about working on Sunday, especially when something happens during the hazy beer-addled halftime of the Super Bowl. I would like to think that perhaps some of the slowness was due to the fact that they didn't want to cover something as lame as a boob popping out on live TV, but judging from the events of the following days, I would be wrong.

This whole ordeal began back in February of 2003. NFL Commissioner Paul Tagliabue announced that Janet Jackson would be performing during the halftime of Super Bowl XXXVIII. "We are pleased that a star like Janet Jackson will join the roster of entertainers who have made the Super Bowl Halftime so special." No doubt he regrets the statement now. It might not have been too bad if not for the fact that they also invited Justin Timberlake, aka the Wardrobe Malfunction Enabler. Kind of like a party enabler, except with, you know, wardrobe malfunctions.

During an otherwise completely forgettable Super Bowl halftime show, Justin Timberlake and Janet Jackson were performing on stage when Timberlake performed a dance move that resulted in part of Janet Jackson's costume popping off. This revealed her right breast, along with a gigantic piercing in the shape of a star or a sun or something. If you squinted really close, you could just barely make out a nipple. Maybe. Most people thought it was a pastie, at least initially. The implication being, if it had been a pastie, things would have been fine, sans nipple. Which I doubt.

Note that an event of national media significance was launched because of the live broadcast on network TV of less than a quarter of an inch of nipple being uncovered, an amount of nipple so small that you couldn't really even see it.

Which brings me to one of my favorite two-beers-in rants. On any given night on broadcast TV you can witness the reenactment of dozens of murders. Hundreds if there's a war movie on. Half of all broadcast programming is CSI-type crime dramas where people are stabbed, beaten, raped, and killed throughout the entire show. I once saw an episode of a show on network TV where not one but TWO cadavers appeared with the tops of their heads sheared off and their brains removed. The other half of all broadcast programming is reality TV, where producers strive to give the most airtime to the most damaged people they can find. You don't hear anyone complaining about all the violence, but you put one nipple on TV and all hell breaks loose. A nipple. You can expose the entire rest of the breast, you can show women taking their shirts off facing the other way. But don't you DARE show that little dot of different-colored flesh that you can plainly see standing at attention anytime Jennifer Aniston appears on *Friends* reruns. The only difference being that on *Friends* hers are shirt-colored.

A couple of years ago I was driving around Louisville, Kentucky, listening to an NPR-type call-in show of some kind. Someone called up to complain about professional wrestling and how much it had changed since she was young. The talk show host agreed. She said she couldn't hardly let her children watch it anymore because things had gotten so out of control. The talk show host agreed. Then she got down to the crux of her problem with it: too much sex. What? The talk show host agreed. Apparently depicting men beating the ever-living shit out of each other wasn't the problem; it was the gals wearing bikinis who would show up from time to time to advance the soap opera–like plot. And there weren't even nipples involved.

So let's recap. Killing, fine. Rape, fine. Display every other part of the breast, fine. Show nipples through cloth material, fine. People eating live insects to win prizes, fine. Nipples? Not fine.

At any rate, the actual event—Jackson's nipple's appearance— was pretty much over before it started. Now all that remained was media outrage.

We've discussed how any given incident will garner about a day's worth of attention, maybe three if it's a crime involving a court case. The Jackson Wardrobe Malfunction ate up a full week of nonstop media coverage. At the time, since Fark first started, this was the most media coverage given to anything other than 9/11. Usually stories persist because of mitigating factors; in this case we really had only one: celebrity involvement. So why the flood of coverage?

I think the answer is twofold. One, it involved boobies. The media loves to talk about the boobies. Whether it's Jennifer Lopez wearing a boobie-revealing dress to the Grammys, so-and-so posing nude for *Playboy*, Paris Hilton's sex tape leaking out, the annual release of the *Sports Illustrated* Plausible Deniability T&A, I mean, Swimsuit Issue. It's because over half the media audience (most males, some females) loves hearing about boobies. The other reason the story was in Mass Media so long is moral outrage. People who don't love the boobies love to get mad about them. I think there was also a bit of The Media Loves to Hate Itself thrown in for good measure, or in this case everyone else bashing the hell out of CBS for letting the stunt happen in the first place.

For whatever reason, people were definitely interested. It was the most replayed moment in TiVo history, which had the unfortunate side effect of publicizing the fact that TiVo has a way to find out exactly how many times you've watched "Filthy Sluts Go to Whoretown" this week. That caused a mini media firestorm by itself.

So what happened next?

The BBC ran a story the following Monday on the debacle, trying to explain to its audience why the hell anyone in America even cared. "Two seconds of bare flesh and America is beside itself with indignation and outrage." The incident had "left the U.S. in a state of mass apoplexy on the subject of decency and taste in broadcasting." Did I mention that every episode of *Fear Factor* involves contestants having to eat live insects, worms, or something equally disgusting? "'That was the most disgusting thing I have ever seen at a sports spectacle,' said baseball coach Tommy Lasorda." A nipple? Surely one of the bench-clearing brawls Lasorda's been involved in over his baseball career had to rate higher. Such as little kids crying in the stands as their sports heroes beat each other senseless. Farker SmiteTheRighteous rightly complained that "a bared breast on national television, America screams and the FCC demands an investigation the next day. Faulty wartime intelligence, and you have to practically bribe your government to get them to investigate."

The BBC also pointed out (hey, a pun) that the nipple appeared during the Super Bowl, which also featured multiple commercials for erectile dysfunction drugs and at least one advertisement involving a flatulent horse. The lack of complaints over the erectile dysfunction drug commercials particularly confuses me because the commercials were about as blatant as you could get. You'd see a guy looking disheartened, his wife upset; then he'd take the drug and you absolutely know the very next thing he was going to do once the commercial was over.... Or so the commercials implied.

So with all this going on during commercial breaks in the Super Bowl, the U.S. media was bent out of shape because of the nipple. Don't even get me started on the commercial, aired during that same Super Bowl, with the flatulent horse. No complaints voiced about that either. I have a complaint, though; my two-year-old ran around the house for a week afterward making farting noises.

There's some debate as to whether the big Janet Jackson boob reveal was on purpose or not. Moments after it happened, Timberlake somehow ran into a reporter from *Access Hollywood* and told him, "Hey, man, we love giving you all something to talk about." Matt Drudge claimed on his Web site DrudgeReport.com to have information that proved CBS execs had even OKed the stunt in advance. I could certainly see it; Jackson's choice of nipple jewelry is pretty suspect considering what she was doing at the time. Let's say you know you're going to be onstage dancing around wildly for fifteen minutes and you have a nipple piercing. Do you put in the stud, or do you put in the five-pound two-inch-wide metal Celtic sun? Me, I'd pick the stud, but I don't have pierced nipples, so what do I know?

My favorite article came from *The Scotsman*, an online Scottish newspaper. Did you know that Liverpool resident Mark Roberts managed to strip down buck-ass naked and streak the same Super Bowl? Yeah, no one else saw it either.

You've probably seen a picture of this guy from one of his streaks at a golf event where he's running away from two cops, and on his back someone has written "19th hole" with an arrow pointing to his crack. Roberts holds the Guinness World Records title of Most Prolific Streaker, mainly at European sporting events.

Roberts ran out onto the field and did a jig from *Riverdance,* complete with a moonwalk. He was then tackled hard by New England Patriots linebacker Matt Chatham. Hardly anyone heard about it. Which was the crux of the article; the poor streaker was complaining that all the media publicity over Janet had blown him right out of the media spotlight. He'd been hired by Golden Palace, which up until that time had been hiring streakers with its Web site address in obvious display on their bodies. During the game the announcers did mention there was a disturbance on the field but didn't say what it was. Most people aren't aware of this, but American sports media intentionally doesn't give attention to people pulling these high jinks. The theory is, ignoring them will cut down on the number of people doing these things.

By Wednesday, Mass Media was scraping the bottom of the barrel for something boobie-related to talk about. Luckily for them, someone filed a class-action lawsuit. Terri Carlin, a Knoxville bank employee—and apparently in no way related to George Carlin if she was offended by a dot of a nipple appearing onscreen—filed a class-action suit again Janet Jackson, Justin Timberlake, CBS, MTV, Viacom, and for all I know, God, Jesus, the Holy Spook, and all the rice in China. Carlin charged that Jackson's exposure and sexually explicit conduct by other performers on the show had injured viewers. The Smoking Gun had the best riff on the lawsuit: "An exact dollar figure is not specified. But it seems billions would be in order since Carlin notes that punitive damages should not exceed the gross revenues of all defendants for the past three years." The lawsuit was dropped five days later. At least one Farker was disappointed; car_go_fast expressed regret that he could not file a class-action defamation of character lawsuit against Terri Carlin for making Americans look like a bunch of prudish, litigious asshats. He indicated that he would simply wait to file it until some fat person sued McDonald's over their food.

Incidentally, Jackson appeared topless on an album she released two months later. Shocking, I know.

The media coverage of the Jackson debacle lasted a little over a week, which was far, far too long. It's possible that it was stretched out a bit due to the fact that Jackson was supposed to perform at the Grammys in a Luther Vandross tribute a week later. Perhaps the media was drooling in anticipation of a repeat of some kind. Jackson was subsequently uninvited, although Timberlake still went. I guess he was deemed OK, since he was the boob-er and not the boob-ie.

After a week of articles, the last of which was the announcement that the class-action lawsuit had been dropped, Farkers were practically screaming for it to just fucking stop. I was right there with them. There may have been some articles about the incident that appeared later but I refused to post them on Fark. There are only so many ways to analyze a situation that involves a boob. Media coverage by this point was starting to resemble a Beavis and Butt-Head skit. "Heh heh heh BOOBIES heh heh." "Uh huh huh uh huh, you said 'BOOBIES.' Uh huh huh."

Sadly, the Janet Jackson incident will be with us forever. What should have been an otherwise completely forgettable piece of performance pop-art trash now lives in infamy, to be endlessly brought up and discussed before Every. Single. Super. Bowl. Ever. For the rest of time, or at least until Mass Media stops giggling about nipples like five-year-olds discovering their first curse words.

Mass Media literally gets stuck in these reporting cycles sometimes. It's as if they have no idea how to stop it. It happens near constantly during slow news periods. Remember Mel Gibson's anti-Jewish tirade after being pulled over by the cops? Terell Owens doing pretty much anything? Representative Mark Foley sending vulgar instant messages to sixteen-year-old congressional pages? Gary Condit? Muslims rioting for weeks over Danish political cartoons? E. coli in bagged spinach? Media Fatigue events pop up continually and make us all want to claw our eyes out. The trick is, just hang in there and wait for the magical words "Has the Media Gone Too Far?" Then take a deep breath and relax, because it's finally over. Until the next thing happens.

Lesser Media Space Fillers

AFTER HAVING READ LITERALLY HUNDREDS OF THOUSANDS OF Mass Media articles, I've noticed there are quite a few other more minor variants of crap that Mass Media uses to fill space. For example, every year or so the wire services run an article on German condom sizes being too large for their population. I don't know if this is a company issuing a press release this year or not. I doubt it, because who would want to annoy the entire nation of Germany by saying they have small dicks? Other than France, that is.

I'm fairly positive that there isn't a news editor out there with the expressed intent of running every Germans Have Small Penises story they come across. Somehow these stories get press anyhow. There are certain types of stories very familiar to journalists and the reading public alike that we've all seen hundreds of times. Some of these you'll probably recognize, others may be new to you.

MISSING WHITE WOMEN

Missing white chicks. I used to argue that it was missing hot chicks until the summer of 2005 when a hot black chick went missing. No national media coverage ensued. *USA Today* ran a follow-up article on this phenomenon, citing a study showing that most missing person articles are indeed about missing white girls. Within days of this study being published, a media frenzy ensued for a week over three missing Puerto Rican boys. Then Mass Media went back to covering stories on missing white chicks.

This type of story floods the news for days on end anytime it occurs. One particular story probably would have gotten play for the category it represents but received press coverage far disproportionate to other Missing White Women stories because it happened in Atlanta. It's a bit of an intersection with another Lesser Media Space Filler, Proximity to NYC and, in this case, CNN hub Atlanta.

A friend of mine who works for CNN recalls that after 9/11, CNN (and for that matter, Mass Media in general) proclaimed that things had changed. They pledged to focus more on harder news stories, the important meaty issues of the day. Just three years later, he was woken up at the crack of 2:00 A.M. on a Monday to come in for something urgent. He thought it was something amazingly important. Instead, it was a blazing sign from the heavens that the media had gone back to its old ways.

Jennifer Wilbanks didn't like her fiancé. She also had some unspecified people in her life who were trying to exhibit an unspecified amount of control on her life. That's nearly exactly how she stated it; what that all means is anyone's guess.

Four days before her wedding, she disappeared from Duluth, Georgia. Mass Media went batshit crazy over it. Hence, missing white chicks are big news. Then came the twist: Three days after her disappearance, Wilbanks called her family to tell them that she was in New Mexico and that she had been abducted and sexually assaulted by a Hispanic male and a white woman.

Just like Bugs Bunny, Wilbanks was about to take a wrong turn at Albuquerque.

It turns out she made the whole thing up. After being questioned by police officers, she eventually admitted to having fabricated the entire story. This ended up landing her a felony charge, which was later plea-bargained to two years probation and a bunch of community service. Part of her community service was mowing lawns, though personally I don't think that should count. She also had to pay $2,250 to the local sheriff's department for their BS-related expenses. I think she got off pretty light there as well.

Now why in hell this demanded more than a passing media mention is beyond me. Mass Media went on for two weeks about the Runaway Bride; the amount of coverage was nearly suffocating. Name a talk show, she was on it. Come to think of it, so were her family and sixteen bridesmaids. (Sixteen??) Hollywood bought the rights to her story as well. Book deals were handed out to everyone involved in the ordeal who was at least semiliterate. Media coverage was completely out of control, to the point where an Atlanta hockey team had Runaway Bride Bobblehead Giveaway Night. The first 1,000 people received a free Jennifer Wilbanks bobblehead complete with stamped bus ticket to Albuquerque.

One of the items on Fark's long list of Things We're Probably Responsible For but Can't Prove was a Scripps Howard study on media coverage of missing person cases. Even before the Runaway Bride burst onto the scene, it was a Fark cliché to link to articles about hot missing white chicks. Before reading this study I was under the impression that Mass Media really was concerned just with hot chicks, but it turns out there's a definite racial bias in play. Moreover, it turns out there's a definite age bias, with white girls under twelve getting more attention than any other demographic.

The study then turned its attention to missing children stories only. They reviewed 43 stories reported by CNN and 162 stories reported by the AP over four years. The results for the AP: 67 percent of missing children stories were about white children. The results for CNN: 76 percent of missing children stories were about white children.

It's interesting to note that shortly after this study came out, Mass Media gave an inordinate amount of coverage to three missing Hispanic boys, who sadly were found dead days later. Then, never again. I can't recall the last time I saw a main-page headline story on a missing person who wasn't female and white. I'm not arguing that it hasn't happened and I didn't see it, I'm saying that Mass Media was caught with its pants down, briefly tried to rectify the problem, then went back to its old ways.

Amusingly, Wilbanks and her fiancé stayed engaged after the event. For another year. Personally I think a gal who creates a story that kicks off a national manhunt to get out of marrying ME would be a huge warning sign reading "I AM BATSHIT INSANE." But that's me. I don't like them crazy. I realize some guys do; they're welcome to them.

OH MY GOD, SOMEONE HAS TRANSLATED THE BIBLE INTO SLANG. AGAIN.

Martin Luther is widely credited with breaking up the Catholic Church, something that happened by complete accident. He hadn't intended to do it; he wanted to reform the church. Politics intervened, and everything went to crap. There, I've just summed up the entire Reformation for all you non-history buffs out there.

Turns out that the title of Guy Who Started the Reformation should belong to John Wycliffe, who did the unthinkable: He translated the Bible into English. In the Middle Ages, church services were held only in Latin, and the Bible was still written only in Latin. Aside from the small stumbling block that most people in medieval Europe were illiterate, most of them couldn't understand Latin either, especially when read to them at church services. Wycliffe decided to fix this by translating the Bible into English. This earned the consternation of the Catholic Church, which declared the translation to be "unauthorized" and later declared that the Bible couldn't be translated unless the Church specifically allowed it.

The general reaction to Wycliffe's translation is our next Lesser Known Media Bias: Always print stories about yahoos translating the Bible into slang. Be it ebonics, spanglish, or any other global vernacular, articles about Bible translation are written to elicit an "oh my God, how could they do that" reaction from the audience, particularly the old folks who are already convinced the world is going to hell. Another hallmark of this type of article is a section where the authors of the translation say they did it to convert the godless heathens of the target culture.

These articles are particularly easy to write because at least half of the writing for them can be direct cut-and-paste quotes from the translated work. These exist solely for humor value to the reading audience, as in "Ha-ha, look at those stupid [insert culture here], they sure talk stupid."

Case in point, a sample article: In order to bring JEEEEzusss to the godless in Australia, the Bible first has to be translated into Aussiespeak:

> "THERE was this sheila who came across a snake-in-the-grass with all the cunning of a con man. The snake asked her why she didn't just grab lunch off the tree in her garden.
>
> "God, she said, had told her she'd be dead meat if her fruit salad came from that tree, but the snake told her she wouldn't die. So she took a good squiz and then a bite and passed the fruit on to her bloke. Right then and there, they'd realised what they'd done and felt starkers."

So begins the biblical account of the fall of mankind retold using "strine," or Australian vernacular.

The article wastes the first half pulling various quotes from various sections, the "Ha-ha, those Australians sure talk funny" kind of quotes. The article's author briefly interviews the translation's author, who, oblivious to the derogatory slant of these types of articles, defends the Australian language (yes, he says language) as being a "language of the heart."

That's really all there is to it; most of the article space is copy-and-paste fluff.

» Last One Left

For Bruce so loved the world, that he gave his only begotten Son, that whosoever believeth in him should not perish, but have everlasting life. No poofters.
Bruce 3:16

» Doggie McNugget

"And Jesus broke the billawompus and and said 'eat of this, for it's my body that I have dingledinkumed for you'"

» Strangeguitar

You call that a crown of a thorns?
  This is a crown of thorns.

» RocketRod

Put another Savior on the crucifix for ya, mate?
  Jesus . . . it's Australian for Salvation.

» ChairmanKaga

Oeyy, take this beer, for its me blood. The blood of the new and everlasting
deal. Brake a deal, face the wheel.

» NittLion78

"Theh ah some 'oo think Chroist put 'is digiridoo in a sheila named Mary
Magdalene."

» GodsTumor

The dingo got my baby jebus!

» Wingnutx

And Jesus said to his new disciple, "Are you not called Bruce? That's going
to cause a bit of confusion!"

» Bondith

"And the Lord said 'Eat, for this is my body,' and we all said 'Strewth, mate,
this could use a bit of Vegemite.'"

» Allanhowls

In the beginnin' was fark-all, then The Big Guy had a piss-up and said,
"Loit!" And at the end of the dai, there was loit. And it was fair dinkum.
Too right.

SHARK ATTACKS

We're fascinated with wild animals that can kill us. In the conti-
nental United States we've pretty much all but eliminated the

major carnivores, not that there were that many to begin with. We hear about people getting eaten by lions in Africa, but that doesn't happen around here. Incidentally the most lethal animal in Africa is the hippopotamus. Those things are mean and nasty, which explains why you've never seen a herd of them on an African farm. Just imagine the size of those hippo steaks, though. Mmm, hippo steaks.

Since there aren't any carnivores, we have to settle for animals that kill us accidentally, like bears or snakes. Contrary to popular belief, snakes aren't trying to kill people to eat them, they're trying to get the hell out of the way. Past that, we have people who are killed when they hit deer with cars, but that doesn't excite anyone. It's not like they're jumping out in front of cars to kill you, although my dad, who lives in north central Pennsylvania, will argue differently. In his neck of the woods they have some of the highest car insurance rates in the nation, mainly due to cars hitting deer. That hardly inspires fear on a national scale.

But sharks, now there's something different. Sharks are probably the only carnivorous creature that could possibly kill someone in the United States. It turns out this is an exceedingly rare occurrence. That doesn't keep Mass Media from reporting every damn time someone even sees a shark at a beach, much less every time someone gets attacked by one. We could blame *Jaws*, or *Shark Week* on the Discovery Channel, or any other number of things as to why Shark Attacks get so much media coverage. It's most likely due to the fact that getting attacked by a shark is a fascinating way to die.

The worst I ever saw it was spring and summer of 2001. Shark stories were hitting Mass Media like nobody's business. This was probably due to the fact that nothing was going on other than the Gary Condit/Chandra Levy thing. For months it was Condit and Shark Attacks on main pages of newspapers everywhere. This came to a screeching halt for obvious reasons after September 10, 2001.

Every year there is still a preponderance of Shark Attack articles. It's interesting to note that most of them appear in the springtime. Shark Attacks are spread out into the fall; they just aren't reported as often once summer is over. This is due to either Media Fatigue or the fact that no journalists are preparing any beach vacations in October.

I don't expect Shark Attack articles will stop anytime soon. For one thing, it is sort of important to know if sharks have been spotted on your local beach. Aside from that, it's a great go-to story for when news simply isn't happening. Of course the Shark Attack stories tend to dry up completely when real news makes an appearance.

HURRICANES

My wife's grandmother is a permanent Florida resident. Every year if we're visiting during the late summer she shows us one of her projects: tracking every single hurricane in the gulf. This is very similar to something my dad does; in particular he likes to track box scores at Red Sox games. Every morning she gets out her photocopied map of the gulf and plots the path of every named storm. Sometimes this gets to be quite a chore. In 2005, the map looked like a deranged two-year-old had gotten ahold of numerous colored pens and scrawled all over her map, with all points ending in Florida.

It makes perfect sense to me why she, or any other Florida resident for that matter, does this. Florida gets pounded by hurricanes constantly, so badly that there's a huge mandatory deductible on home insurance premiums. If I were in the direct path of hurricanes, I'd probably track them too.

Mass Media loves a good hurricane. Unfortunately they don't

have much in the way of variation on the coverage. It roughly breaks down into the following:

1. Storm gets a name; this means it's bad.

2. Storm wanders toward the U.S., probably heading toward Florida. Usually Cuba gets it as well. How those poor bastards survive in their nineteenth-century state I'll never know.

3. Media begins predicting where the hurricane will land. Special emphasis is given to those that actually might hit the United States (and other places where Americans might frequently vacation). The rest are all but ignored.

4. As hurricanes near the U.S. coastline, Mass Media begins evacuation coverage. News teams are dispatched to go hang out on beaches and show us that the waves are really high and the wind is really strong.

5. Hurricane hits. On-the-spot news teams go stand out in the wind and rain to show just how strong it is. Oooo, sure is windy.

6. Show the eye of the hurricane passing over.

7. Damage assessment. Fly around in helicopters and take pictures of damage. Broadcast pictures for hours.

8. Malign government officials for "Not Having Been Ready."

9. Cover cleanup attempts for a day or two.

10. Get the hell out of Dodge; go back to broadcasting stories about Missing White Women.

Regarding sending news teams right straight into the storm's path, I highly suspect this is why so many people choose to stay in the paths of hurricanes. When you see someone like Willard Scott or Al Roker broadcasting from the most likely point of landfall telling people to evacuate, it's kind of hard to take them seriously. After all, they don't appear to be worried about anything.

PLANE CRASHES (OR ANYTHING PLANE-RELATED)

It doesn't matter how big the plane is or where in the world it happens, this is news. For some damn reason.

I know dozens of people personally who are afraid to fly. I can't help but think that it's because of the constant national media exposure of plane crashes. The truth is, they simply don't happen that often. When they do happen, it rarely involves commercial aircraft. When it does involve commercial aircraft, people are rarely killed. Compare and contrast this to the number of times you or someone you know have been in car accidents.

I don't know if this is the fault of 9/11 or not, but you could have an ultralight go down in Topeka and it would make national news. Mass Media is flat-out fascinated with plane crashes for some reason. I don't get it. It's not like this is new technology. This isn't 1910, where we're all smacking our foreheads in amazement that a heavier-than-air machine can take off and fly us straight to Timbuktu and get us there in less than five weeks. Perhaps there's some part of the human psyche that just can't believe in flying metal juggernauts.

PENIS AMPUTATIONS. OR JUST ABOUT ANYTHING ELSE TO DO WITH PENISES . . . PENI? PENII?

Mass Media loves a good dick joke . . . er, article.

Somewhere in the world at least once a week someone gets his penis cut off. Usually this is done by a current or ex significant other. Occasionally it's done by the owner himself. Strange variations of this include getting it caught in a toilet seat lid or having it glued to one's thigh by a jilted lover. Just recently we've been seeing articles about guys getting their nutsacks caught in the slats of wooden chairs.

If you think about it, it's odd that penis amputations receive so much coverage. No other amputation gets this kind of press. People cut their arms and legs off all the time and we never hear about it. If someone cuts a boob off we never hear about it either, which honestly is fine by me. When a guy does that to a woman, everyone assumes he is sick and twisted. When a woman cuts off a guy's wang, everyone assumes he probably had it coming.

Here's a disturbing example of a penis-related story that shouldn't have seen the light of day.

Both prosecuting and defense attorneys in penis-pump trial found it necessary to display their prowess at air masturbation in court for the jury.

For the sake of making this section less grisly, I went with one of the more unique penis-related stories of our time: the Penis-Pumping Judge.

Former judge Donald D. Thompson, who when he dies will

probably end up with the words "Penis Pump" somewhere in his newspaper obituary, was brought to trial on charges that he used a penis pump in his courtroom. On himself. During actual cases. Multiple times. In plain sight of witnesses and the court reporter, who testified that she saw him use it fifteen times on himself between 2001 and 2003. When he was brought up on charges, Thompson's defense was that it was a gag gift from a friend and he never used it in the courtroom, despite several eyewitness accounts and even pictures.

The main thrust of the article was describing numerous courtroom shenanigans that received uproarious laughter from the jury. One such scene involved a urologist expert witness who said he "still used those" when asked if it was an outdated form of treatment. "Not you personally?" asked the attorney. "No," said the urologist. I'm sure it was way funnier in person; nothing translates worse to the written word than a retelling of a penis joke. The article even opens with a description of how, a number of times, both attorneys on the case had to pantomime masturbation. One of the witnesses, a juror, said he identified the device because he saw it used in movies. Sure, man, whatever you say.

At the time, this article received way more airtime than it should have, considering the subject matter. It was on the front page of CNN every time the case came up, from when charges were handed down to when the trial started to the sentencing. Why? Penis. Ha. Gets a laugh every time.

» AntiNorm

He recommends jacking off as a treatment for erectile dysfunction? Suuuuuuuuuuuure.

» NYU Orthodontics

They aren't for "jacking off" . . . they pull blood into the penis to create an erection. It's not just a joke from Austin Powers . . . these have been a medical device for decades.

I know because I'm in the medical profession, not because I use one. Because I don't. Really. Honest. I don't.

/seriously

/stop looking at me like that

» **Poughdrew**

I can't wait for the Law and Order remake.

» **Ksac3**

He broke the penal code.

» **Alegria**

It took waaaay too long to get to the first "hung jury" joke. I'm ashamed of you guys.

PROXIMITY TO NYC (FOLLOWED BY LA/DC/ATLANTA)

Recently my family and I were visiting my wife's grandmother at her home in Florida. Like most people who grew up on farms, she wakes up around five or six every morning. She starts her day with some coffee and a little morning TV. I recently asked her why she watched the local Tampa Fox affiliate rather than *Good Morning America*, whose demographic as far as I can tell appears to consist entirely of people over a century old (she's not in that demographic, by the way). Her answer: "They spend too much time talking about New York."

Interestingly, similar patterns exist in other countries. Canadian media seems to think everything happens in Toronto. British media pays an inordinate amount of attention to London. South African media, when not writing about fantastic creatures or witch doctors with bad advice, spends most of its time writing about events in Johannesburg. And so on.

The fact remains that most people in the United States, 300 million Americans, do not live in New York. They don't know about the latest media slap fight between the *Daily News* and the *New York Post*, they don't engage in daily debate about the Mets and the Yankees, they don't pepper their words with Yiddish phrases, and they don't take mass transit to work. They also wouldn't know a good hot dog if it bit them on the ass, their home mortgages are a quarter of what New Yorkers pay in rent, their local elementary school yards aren't completely paved, and their air-conditioning actually works during the summer. The differences are enormous. Some would say insurmountable.

Granted, a lot of events do actually take place in New York City. I've lived there myself. One summer during college I witnessed firsthand exactly how huge New York City is. It happened about ten miles from the Jackson Heights brownstone I was living in at the time. A huge ship with hundreds of Chinese refugees wrecked on a beach somewhere in Queens. Mass chaos ensued as the police responded to what was certain to be a huge humanitarian crisis. The refugees, no doubt hoping to escape their horrible lives working for pennies a day in Chinese sweatshops, had paid someone a fortune to smuggle them into the United States, where they would eventually make nearly a dollar a day working in illegal New York sweatshops. If I were in the same position, I would have had them take me to San Francisco. Taking a boat from China to New York has to be at least twice as far.

When the boat wrecked on the shore, everyone made a run for it; hundreds of people came ashore, and the police managed to capture eight of them. The others disappeared without a trace. New York absorbed hundreds of Chinese refugees at the drop of a hat and no one could tell any different the next day. Not that many cities are capable of doing that. I remember riding the 7 train the next day, looking around wondering who, if anyone, on the subway car had been on the boat the night before. There was no way to tell ...

As amazing as New York City is, and regardless of what its inhabitants think, it is simply not the center of the United States. So why then does Mass Media give so much airtime to New York events? Because all they have to do is walk outside to find a story. Stick a camera out the window, roll film. That and most of the news correspondents actually live there, giving that extra edge to stories because the stories affect them personally. It's one thing when a building explodes in Peoria, it's another thing entirely when it explodes down the street.

This would explain why in 2003, when a power outage hit most of the northeastern United States and parts of Canada, and by northeastern I mean as far west as Ohio, the vast majority of the coverage of the several-thousand-mile-wide event was about what was going on in Manhattan. It did sound like one hell of a party.

Proximity to New York City is compounded by the fact that news media, especially TV news media, love to go off the script into breaking news. They're ready to go at the drop of a hat, literally. It's what they live for. A friend of mine who works for CNN says it's great, because all the producers kick back and start compiling information coming in. It's fast, exciting, and full of extended smoke breaks when it's something not too terribly important. Most of all, it's easy to cover in person. What's not to like?

It was hard to pick just a few examples, as this happens all too frequently.

Three-story building collapse in Manhattan. No word on when Mass Media plans to give front page coverage to building collapses in Kansas, Iowa.

On a busy Tuesday morning, as if there are any other kinds of mornings in Manhattan, a building on 62nd Street between Park and Madison avenues collapsed. Now certainly this was a tragedy, because people were almost killed. Actually one man *was* killed, the guy who set off the explosion in the first place. He was mad at his ex-wife, who won the building in a divorce settlement, so he figured he'd just blow it up, himself along with it. Genius. I would like to point out that there are much better ways of getting back at your ex-wife than that.

In a tragedy of a different sort, Mass Media devoted practically the rest of the entire day to live coverage of the exploded building. Three hours of smoking wreckage footage during morning coverage followed by significant play the rest of the day, and front page articles the following morning. The tagline on Fark claimed that if the building had been in the middle of nowhere, there would have been no media coverage.

In the thread, annoyed New Yorkers argued that this was not the case, and that Mass Media would give equal coverage if something similar happened elsewhere in the U.S. Except that it had already happened earlier that morning.

Another building explodes, this time in northern Wisconsin. Scoreboard: Two people missing, no national network news footage.

In Ellison Bay, Wisconsin, at about two in the morning that same day, a gas main exploded, destroying three buildings and killing two people. It wasn't completely ignored by Mass Media, but coverage amounted to a passing mention.

Manhattan Farkers argued that their building explosion was more important, because it impacted traffic and potentially inconvenienced hundreds of thousands of people. What, by making them have to travel an extra block if on foot, two if by car? The Wisconsin explosion caused considerably more damage, literally and figuratively. The building was a hotel, the only one in the small town. This succeeded in killing off what little tourist industry the town had, and damn near erased the entire town from the map for lack of outside income. The only argument New Yorkers had left at the end of the day was "Who cares about Wisconsin?" And that's exactly my point.

» NikolaiFarkoff

If it happens in NYC, it's automatically assumed to be terrorism.

» Palexc

Exactly. Not by NY'ers though. "Explosion" in anything less than a skyscraper automatically means gas leak to most people.

» Albo

It was a cruise missile.

» Loabn

The media is making up for the lack of coverage they gave NYC after the last time a building collapsed.

» I_C_Weener

Hang on a second, submitter. Are you saying that Kansas and Iowa have real 3 story buildings? i think you are reaching here.

» Walking Carpet

All the news outlets are trying really, really hard to tie this imagery to 9/11, pretty pathetic.

I think I even saw on FoxNews "IT SOUNDED LIKE A BOMB" as a graphic. Everybody panic.

» I_C_Weener

How many of these are happening each day? How many are the liberal press hiding from us?

Storm leaves 450,000 St. Louis residents without power as temperatures threaten to pass 100 degrees. If this had been in New York City, you would have already heard about it. Constantly.

St. Louis was absolutely nailed one summer by a massive storm system. Buildings collapsed, freeways were shut down, and hundreds of thousands of people went without power for days during one of the worst heat waves the city had ever seen. It was an absolute nightmare.

We posted an initial article on Fark. It linked to a regular article covering the storm devastation in St. Louis, but a debate soon ensued in the article comments due to confusion as to what the point of the tagline was. The tagline wasn't insinuating that the story was getting no coverage, it was that it wasn't getting as much as it would if the same thing happened in New York City. The problem was, the argument was pretty much hypothetical. We couldn't back up the assertion. Until the following day.

Fark prophecy comes true: more press coverage given to New York power outage affecting far fewer people than to St. Louis power outage caused by devastating storms.

At the time the article posted to Fark, Con Ed still wasn't sure what exactly was causing the NYC blackouts. New York was receiving similar hot weather, and since the population density there is a bit higher, it could just have been that the grid was overloaded, something the Con Ed spokesman in the article was unwilling to put under consideration, at least in front of TV cameras. It was probably for legal issues or something; either that or it's a by-product of the same complex suffered by telcos, cable companies, electric companies, and governments everywhere. Specifically, they go out of their way to avoid saying anything is their fault, especially when they know it really is their fault.

In New York, 25,000 people were without power, according to Con Ed. The amount of press coverage given to this story, particularly by the TV networks, was FAR in excess of the coverage given to the St. Louis disaster. I would argue that neither event was particularly compelling; both stories should have received a normal amount of coverage. St. Louis did receive a normal amount of coverage. New York City, on the other hand, received intense, blistering media spotlight attention, occupying far more of the news day than the St. Louis disaster. Given that far more people were affected in St. Louis, surely a much larger percentage of Fox News's audience would be likely to be affected by the St. Louis disaster. Except for the fact that none of them could really watch Fox News until the power came back on. Which didn't happen until long after the New York power outage was wrapped up.

The New York outage didn't receive more coverage because it was the more recent story. Both power outages hit on the same day, but Mass Media didn't figure it out until a day after it happened. Five days later, Mass Media was still spending more time and resources on the New York story.

» Mordant

Well, people in NYC are accustomed to having electricity.

» NikolaiFarkoff

I'm glad it's St. Louis and not NY/LA . . . because then we'd have to hear the incessant "global warming" spiel instead of the more appropriate "shiat happens" spiel.

» NPComplete

Yeah, but if it hit New York then people would have been affected. Human people!

» Oldfarthenry

If it was Ontario, it would be business as usual.
    "Oh, the hydro's out. Let's play with our flashlights."

» Monkeystealsthepeach

No shiat! Everytime something happens in New York, good or bad, they act like they are the first city it's ever happened to.
    /I'll give them a pass on the big thingy a few years ago.

» MuffDiver

Come on down to Florida and try it out in August after a hurricane zaps your grid for a week.
    Solution? = Alcohol.
    /get it before the ice melts. . . .

» Folding_bike

New Yorkers think we are the center of the universe because we are. Just look at any universe map.

» Shrugging Atlas

What's funny is the baseball stadium (in St. Louis) had power last night and they managed to get in the game, albeit a few hours late. Bonus points for still serving beer during the entire delay!

The airport? Shut down all night due to lack of power.

» ChicoEscuela

What is this St. Louis you speak of?

» Glassa

And if the roof of LaGuardia Airport flew off and landed on a major highway, it would be all over the news.

Roof flew off part of Lambert Airport and landed on I-70 in St. Louis! Try beating that for shiat happening in your area!

Obliviousness to surrounding areas isn't indigenous to New York only. Several springs ago, the first storm front of the season ripped through Kentucky. This is always very exciting, especially for local meteorologists who get to take over the live network feed for an hour to wax poetic about the various colors occupying the local weather radar map. You'll notice they usually don't do this for the second storm front, and certainly not the third. In recent years they've taken to relegating live radar pictures to the bottom corner of the screen so you don't miss any commercials.

This particular year, the local station in question had installed a version of weather radar that detected circulation in clouds. Boy, that sure got the local weather guy excited. "We're seeing some definite circulation here! EVERYBODY PANIC." Circulation in clouds is extremely common, as it turns out; most of the time it doesn't mean anything. However, there was indeed actual reason to panic. One of the dozens of circulation thingees on the weather map was actually a tornado. It tore through a subdivision, wandering through just across the street from my friend Kevin, taking his 100-pound recently refilled propane tank with it and pulling thousands of nails in his roof out about half an inch. Since this didn't count as actual damage as far as the insurance company was concerned, he ended up spending the next few weekends on his roof, putting all the nails back one by one, cursing insurance companies with each swing of the hammer.

By the time the storm, complete with at least two tornadoes, passed through the Lexington area or, more to the point, past the local TV station, live coverage immediately signed off. Danger's over, see you all later. Never mind the fact that there were about forty counties east of Lexington that were pretty damn curious as to where those tornadoes got off to. I can only assume they received a ton of hate mail about it, because now when local TV stations do live coverage, they follow the storms for a good 25–50 miles east of town.

This problem is endemic to any locale with a city large enough to have a decent media presence. I don't know this for a fact but I imagine Oklahomans aren't real fond of Oklahoma City hogging all the local media coverage. People in Wyoming are probably pissed off at some city too. Are there cities in Wyoming? Chicagoans would probably be surprised to learn that there is something other than Chicago occupying the state of Illinois. In fact, some years ago, a Chicago radio station had a jingle: "Just outside of Chicago there's a place called Illinois."

Proximity to New York City certainly isn't some kind of media conspiracy. Mass Media doesn't attend continuing education conferences or take journalism classes where they learn to concentrate only on the cities they live in. They do it because it's easy. And in New York's case they do it because the rest of the U.S. doesn't exist as far as they're concerned. It's not that Mass Media fails to cover stories elsewhere; they do mention them. It's also not to say that stories elsewhere are more important than stories in major U.S. cities. My point is that Mass Media gives

New York/LA/DC/Atlanta stories disproportionate airtime because it's easy.

The city most screwed by this phenomenon is Seattle. If something happens in Seattle after 7:00 P.M. EST on a Friday, no media coverage ensues. I've seen it happen time and time again. No self-respecting East Coast media employee turns the car around, gets back on the subway, or leaves the bar early to head back to work on a Friday evening for anything less than a major catastrophe. Like, say, a tarp fire on the 59th Street Bridge.

MEDIA HEARTS THE MEDIA

Mass Media loves to talk about itself.

Reporters aren't usually experts in scientific fields. They have an hour or so to interview someone with technical knowledge, then have to try to convert this technical knowledge into something a layman can understand. This rarely succeeds.

Mass Media journalists do have one area of expertise, though: They are experts in Mass Media. They can go on about the subject for days and days. Witness the recent glut of coverage given to Weblogs. Weblogs cover media too. Mass Media knows all about that, and thus they pound that topic into the ground well past any regular person's capacity to care about the subject.

Incidentally, this is where the Has the Media Gone Too Far? component of Media Fatigue comes from. In general, once Mass Media gets around to asking Has the Media Gone Too Far? it has. Again, the average person couldn't give a rat's ass; they just want Mass Media to shut the hell up once they've gone too far, not inject any more analysis.

In particular, Mass Media loves to jump all over plagiarists within its own ranks. They're incredibly eager to crap all over these scoundrels who are ruining the reputation of journalists everywhere. It's like blood in the water around sharks.

Andrew Breitbart (of Breitbart.com and the Drudge Report) said something to me once on the subject: You will get more media publicity if you work for Mass Media and plagiarize someone than you will if you are a mass murderer. He's right. Media coverage of plagiarists is far in excess of the actual importance of the story. Additionally, the media seems completely unaware that only they give a shit about this type of article past the first mention. I certainly don't want Mass Media plagiarizing things, but I don't need to read 100 articles about it.

Jayson Blair joined *The New York Times* as an intern in 1998. In 1999 he was hired on as an Intermedia Reporter, whatever the hell that is, and in 2001 he was hired on full-time. In 2003, Blair plagiarized an article from the *San Antonio Express-News*, and Blair resigned soon after. Later it was discovered that he had invented sections of other articles he had written, and plagiarized multiple other times as well. I found all this on Wikipedia by the way, neener neener.

By all rights, that should have been the level of press coverage this event received: one paragraph. Just like the coverage given to accountants who embezzle or attorneys who overbill for their time. These actions negatively impact those professions as well. However, Mass Media controls the coverage level, and they went completely apeshit ballistic. For days and days, Mass Media held vigil, railing at *The New York Times* for allowing such a disgrace in Mass Media to occur.

I suspect at least part of the coverage was a way to indirectly attack *The New York Times* itself, just for the hell of it. This happens often in Mass Media. Take, for example, all the intensive media coverage of perverts on MySpace.com, owned by the same parent company as Fox News. At least part of the motivation for producing those stories is to give Fox News a good whack on the head. Mass Media can't run articles on Fox News sucking without giving the impression that they are petty and vindictive, but they can talk about perverts on MySpace all day long and still appear legitimate. So they do.

Mass Media will respond that media issues are of great importance because they impact the public trust in news organizations. This ignores the fact that most people already believe Mass Media either makes stuff up, is biased one way or the other, or constantly gets information wrong. Finding out that journalists sometimes invent stories just confirms their preexisting viewpoint. A recent CBS News/*New York Times* poll on media trust trumpeted the fact that 63 percent of respondents have a fair amount of confidence in the media. They considered this to be great because it was higher than it had been in recent years. But let us review the answer choices from the poll:

How much confidence do you have in the news media?

A great deal: 15%

A fair amount: 48%

Not very much/None: 36%

Apparently 1 percent were completely baffled by the question.

Mass Media should not celebrate the fact that 48 percent have a "fair amount" of confidence in the news media. A "fair amount" means that they think Mass Media gets it wrong at least some of the time. The poll doesn't examine to what extent the "fair amount" voters thought the media got things wrong, but what level is acceptable? Thinking that Mass Media screws things up half the time? 25 percent of the time? Is 10 percent of the time acceptable?

You could just as easily interpret the poll as saying that 84 percent of respondents think Mass Media screws the pooch at least some of the time, and a decent chunk of those people think Mass Media gets things wrong nearly all of the time. That pretty much speaks for itself.

The same poll also asked the question: The Stories in the News Media are...

Accurate: 69%

Inaccurate: 22%

Sure would have been interesting to break that out a bit more by adding Accurate Most of the Time and Inaccurate Most of the Time.

Either way, it's dangerous for Mass Media to look at numbers like these and proclaim that they are good enough.

Epilogue: What Should Mass Media Be Doing Instead?

WHEN REALLY BAD THINGS HAPPEN, LIKE WARS, FLU OUTBREAKS, the Yankees winning the World Series, and so on, my friends ask me for the 30,000-foot view of What Is Really Going On. All the people I talk to at conventions, Fark parties, or among my own friends are under the impression that they're not being told what is really going on by Mass Media. The truth of the matter is, they're right. Sort of. But not in a tinfoil-hat conspiracy sort of way. Mass Media isn't fabricating news. The information is all there, it's just being emphasized and organized differently, not by importance but by what people are most likely interested in. What people are interested in is not, for the most part, hard news. Witness the travesty that is CNN's most popular articles section. Taking today as a random example, without looking beforehand, mind you, we have a main page story about Bin Laden preparing another attack on the United States. Hey, that's real news. Most popular: "raw fish, air guitar help trio survive 9 months adrift at sea." No further comment needed. This general lack of interest in real, hard news forces Mass Media to take complex topics, distill them to their base components, then overdramatize some facets of them (and not necessarily the appropriate ones either) to draw in eyeballs.

For example, take daily stock market wrap-up reports. After markets close, journalists work on coming up with single-sentence explanations for what happened during the day. "Investors sold stocks broadly today due to (choose one: inflation fears/Hurricane Fred/unrest in the Middle East/rampaging raccoons in Olympia)." And that's it? No one sold stocks for any other reason? In reality there are thousands upon thousands of reasons why stocks go up and down. Describing a large number of the real reasons would take too long, and furthermore most people don't care. It's pointless for Mass Media to try to distill it down to a single explanation because a single explanation can never accurately describe the day's stock market fluctuations. They do so anyhow because it makes a good intro to talking about specific stock moves during the day.

Consider the ramifications of literally hundreds if not thousands of people asking me the question "What news sources do you use to find the real news?" What does this mean? I'm going to go out on a limb here and guess that it means that people suspect they're not getting good information from Mass Media. One of the most obvious indicators for these inquisitive minds would be layouts of Mass Media Web sites, most of which lead with three serious headlines followed up by useless crap such as articles on what David Hasselhoff had to eat for breakfast yesterday and new video of the latest surfing dog they've discovered (or rediscovered). People in general suspect that surely there are more than three important news events happening in the world right this moment that might impact them directly. I'm inclined to agree with that sentiment.

Part of the reason even legitimate news stories have to be punched up is because they're just not all that interesting by themselves. If I had to sum up the state of the world today, I would say that certainly things are bad, but not really any worse than they ever have been. Not very many people believe me on this point.

No one wants to read a news article entitled "Things Are Not All That Bad" (a book that I've wanted to write but which would never ever in a million years sell well). To get people to consume media you have to draw them in somehow, by emphasizing a certain dramatic point to get people to click on the story. Mass Media tries to get people all riled up about how wrong things are by making sweeping generalizations; this is what compels people to consume news. We've made fun of the local newscast saying, "Can this common household product kill you? Find out after this break," but the reason they do it is because it works. Some political pundits' entire careers are built on making off-the-wall statements like "Liberals Are Traitors" and "Conservatives Are Screwing Us All Behind Closed Doors." Now, that's compelling stuff. "Things are OK" isn't motivation enough to get anyone to care, or to buy your paper.

So what should Mass Media be doing instead?

The crux of the problem is similar to my Things Are Not All That Bad book that has no chance in hell of selling. People don't really want to watch or read news that does the right thing. The *McNeil-Lehrer NewsHour* was a great example of this. Quality news, mostly information, and no one watched it. It was dry as toast in a diner at breakfast on Saturday morning. Is there any way to fix this? No. It's also similar to when people complain about no one going to museums, the philharmonic, or opera anymore. The great unwashed masses never did go to those kinds of things (Shakespeare notwithstanding; but remember even Dickens was considered to be pop trash in his day. Kind of makes you wonder what they'll be saying about Stephen King and Dean Koontz in the twenty-second century). These high-end pursuits were, and to a great extent still are, enjoyed by a small wealthy elite. There has never been any broad appeal. They are certainly quality pastimes, but that doesn't mean that everyone, or even most people, should, or can, enjoy them.

The same goes with news. Everyone claims to want real news, but no one really does. The great unwashed masses want the titillation Mass Media provides.

THE FUTURE OF MASS MEDIA

By and large, local Mass Media is screwed. Twenty years ago they were the sole source of news for their respective cities. Today, they are no longer a source of world or national news for the Internet generation. Every year newspaper circulation declines because their subscribers are literally dying off due to old age, and there is no new crop of younger readers coming up behind them. Very few people under the ages of thirty-five to forty purchase newspapers; they get their information almost entirely from the Internet.

Part of the problem confronting mainstream newspapers is that, thanks to deregulation, they effectively became monopolies, got too comfortable (as monopolies do), and stopped innovating. Every large town in the United States used to have at least two newspapers. Then monopoly laws were changed for newspapers, and over the past few decades, local newspapers consolidated. Media markets that once had two or more newspapers now had one. This newly consolidated newspaper entity was the only game in town as far as print media was concerned. They grew far too accustomed to the fact that you pretty much had to buy their product if you wanted to know what was going on.

Once newspapers moved online, most were (and still are) completely oblivious to the fact that they were now all in direct competition with each other, globally. You can read any local newspaper in the world with the click of a mouse button. I say most newspapers were completely unaware because a select few actually were very much aware of the new situation. In particular, some newspapers, such as *The Arizona Republic, The Kansas City Star*, and even a handful of TV stations' Web departments like Local 6 in Orlando and Tampa Bay's 10, quickly realized what they were dealing with and started to make serious moves to differentiate themselves from the pack. The main thing they changed was to make sure their Web sites were not exact duplicates of the newspaper or TV station offerings. They all have loads of original content and features not found in their print and broadcast offerings. The changes have resulted in these media outlets having an Internet presence vastly larger than that of their contemporaries in other larger markets. *Vastly* isn't strong enough a word; these Web sites are literal giants compared to everyone else. What do these media outlets all have in common? Their execs turned their Web departments loose. They said, "We don't understand what the hell it is you're trying to do, but if it works, it works." It works.

Local newspapers may be lulling themselves into false security by thinking they can reverse their subscriber loss somehow, some way. Barring some amazing innovation that no one has yet envisioned, and that's certainly a possibility, print media subscriber loss will not be reversed under any circumstances. A company depending on unheard-of innovation for its survival is about as effective as you depending on the lottery to cover your retirement. In both cases you don't know you're screwed until it's way too late to do anything about it. Media consumers can already find national news from AP and Reuters on Fox News and CNN, which are word-for-word identical to what is available in the local paper. Let me say that again: word-for-word. The same wire services that supply local media with 90 percent of its material are hosted online on thousands of other media Web sites across the Internet, each identical to and as bland as the next.

Local TV is even more screwed than local newspapers. Young folks are going straight to the Internet for TV. YouTube.com, for example, is better than a DVR, because you can find clips of media you didn't even know you wanted to look for. Then once you know you like it, you can seek out the entire show online and download it either from the major network's main Web site or iTunes.

As with local newspapers, you can discount anyone watching local TV news for national news, and as with newspapers, the entire Internet generation is already lost. Local video is the one thing local TV can do better than anyone else. Local TV should be beefing up its Web site offerings and snapping up the local talent that has popped up online out of nowhere in the last few years. They should put all their local video online on demand and have a Web site compelling enough to make people seek them out as an Internet destination. Right now all local TV Web sites look almost alike, which is no accident, because there is one company that builds almost all of them. The use of the same bland, boring layout on practically every TV Web site has pretty much eliminated them from most people's daily Web-browsing patterns.

Local Mass Media that will survive the next decade or two will do so by concentrating on what they do better than anyone else: local news coverage. This is probably a harsh reality for local Mass Media to come to terms with, the fact that their most dangerous competitor is the media-maligned local independent weekly, or even the local popular blogger. In Louisville, for example, former *Courier-Journal* restaurant critic Robin Garr runs his own restaurant review site, LouisvilleHotBytes.com. His site is entertaining and extremely comprehensive, covering practically every restaurant in Louisville and some farther out than that. If I want to know where to eat in Louisville, I go to his site. *The Courier-Journal* might as well mothball their own local restaurant critic as far as I'm concerned; they can't possibly match the kind of in-depth analysis and review that Garr puts out on a consistent basis. In other localities, local bloggers cover local politics, sports, and other events much better than the local Mass Media does.

Why, in a local market where national news is off the table and local news is being done better by others, would anyone pay attention to local Mass Media? For what? People can already read national news on a national news Web site. People already read local politics on their local blogger's site. People can find restaurant reviews and movie listings elsewhere as well, linked directly to where they can make reservations and buy tickets, which is exactly what they want to do when they read a good review. People are already not picking up the local newspaper in hard copy or watching local TV news, but this trend toward national news Web sites leaves them with no compelling reason to check out local Mass Media's Web site either.

If I were local Mass Media, I'd start taking out hits on or, more realistically, buying the guys doing facets of local news better than me before they ran me out of business. I'm talking about the local independent weeklies, bloggers, monthly suburb newsletters, and so on. Just the good ones, not all of them. This has already started happening. *The Boston Globe* noticed that tons of people were going to BostonDirtDogs.com for Red Sox baseball coverage, so they slurped them up. Talk about plausible deniability too: The guy who writes Dirt Dogs can (and does) have a cardiac arrest every time the Red Sox lose, calls the manager and the players every name in the book, and meanwhile his site carries the following disclaimer: "Boston Dirt Dogs is a fan site produced by Boston.com. *The Boston Globe* newspaper and its

Sports Dept. do not oversee the site and have no role in its pro-
duction. BDD's content is solely the responsibility of Boston
.com." Damn, that's nice for *The Boston Globe*. All of the traffic,
none of the responsibility. I'm guessing they've received complaints, hence the disclaimer. Here's the key: It's the very comments that Boston.com receives complaints about that makes
BostonDirtDogs.com, and other similar sites, work. He's un-
apologetic and doesn't give a rat's ass what you think.

National Mass Media is a different situation altogether. They
already have the online audience, they *are* the online destination
where people go to get their syndicated news. Their danger is the
subject of this book, which is whether they lose themselves in this
morass of crap they're cranking out on a daily basis. You can be a
news leader or a crap peddler, not both.

Mass Media needs to further separate the fluff news from the
real. They're torn, however, because it's the fluff that brings the
masses, not the in-depth analyses. In their panic to do "something," some of them have started making extremely stupid decisions that will eventually threaten their very existence. Case in
point: About a year ago the BBC hired some consultants who told
them to redesign the look and feel of its Web site to more resemble
MySpace.com. What. The. Hell? They actually wanted one of the
world's preeminent news sources to dumb itself down to attract
the kids? Would it have worked? Absolutely not. While it's certainly possible they might have attracted a younger demographic,
in doing so they would have shot their reputation for being a reliable news source, right in the back of the head execution-style.
The BBC would soon become the laughingstock of the news industry; no one could take it seriously anymore as a real news
source. Ted Turner is obviously worried about this. He recently
lambasted CNN for doing the same kind of thing, complaining
that its newsroom spent too much time focusing on Pervert of the

Day retrospectives. While Not News does draw eyeballs, it discredits an entire media outlet and its status as a legitimate news organization. In trying to capture both the newshounds and the entertainment fans, Mass Media succeeds in doing neither and losing everything.

The solution for the big guys lies in what happened a few years ago with the emergence of Entertainment News programs. Finally there was a place to put all the useless crap that no respectable media outlet should be talking about. Newspapers have them too; they're called tabloids. As I mentioned in a previous chapter, when I visited *Aftenposten* in Norway a few years back, they told me that their tabloid outsold their actual newspaper by something like ten to one. This is the Mass Media world we live in, and we have always lived in it.

Mass Media outlets have a decision to make: Either embrace the dark side and throw away all pretense of being a serious news media outlet, as some have already done, or retrench and become a leader of real honest-to-god serious information. It turns out there's a way to do both: split off the Not News from the news. Make another Web site, spin off another TV channel. Put all the Not News into another section of the newspaper. Keep it away from the real news. Stop poisoning real news with the kind of spoon-feeding, filler garbage that we've discussed throughout this book.

Let me give you some idea of how difficult a decision this is for Mass Media. Since Fark started in 1999, only two breaking news stories have caused a crush of traffic so high it brought our servers to their knees. The first was 9/11. That's understandable. The other one? Michael Jackson Verdict Reached.

Not Verdict Announced, mind you. Verdict Reached. I think we even blew a hard drive when that happened. Michael Jackson didn't spend a lot of time hanging around at the courthouse during his child molestation trial. He wasn't really in much of a hurry to show up there on time either, something that landed him in contempt of court at least a couple of times. Every chance he got, be it short recess or lunch breaks, he took off. When the jury announced that they had reached a verdict, Jackson was not in the courthouse. He was called by the court and given one hour to get his ass in front of the judge. He made it in just over forty-five minutes.

In that time frame, apparently every Farker on the planet logged on to Fark to see what the verdict was. Things were moving so slowly that I barely was able to get online to post the verdict. This was kind of an embarrassing situation because I'd taken the stance on Fark that the Michael Jackson trial was a complete waste of time that no one cared about. Maybe it should have been, but people evidently did care. Millions of them. And therein lies the problem: The masses would rather read about crap than news. There's nothing wrong with that per se, but if you're a Mass Media outlet trying to present yourself as a serious hard news source, running BREAKING NEWS ALERTs about the pedophile of the week or Mel Gibson's latest DUI arrest is a quick way to disavow media consumers of that notion. Not News drives a ton of traffic.

All that aside, here's the real challenge Mass Media has to overcome down the road: a looming catastrophic drop in advertising income.

I've attended recent conferences where Mass Media has voiced the worry that bloggers will take advertising revenue away from them. Personally I doubt this will happen, at least to any significant degree. There are too many obstacles in the way of the independent blogger, the largest one being getting the attention of mainstream advertisers, who in my experience have the collective intelligence of a sack of wet cats. This impending drop in advertising revenue will come from a completely different heretofore unknown source: accurate advertisement metrics.

One of the most significant paradigm shifts looming for the entire Mass Media industry is that on the Internet we will finally have fairly reliable stats. These accurate statistics will show that the number of people actually SEEING ads while watching video or reading is nowhere near what advertisers have previously been told. Worse still, the conversion rate is far below what salespeople have been telling clients for years. This doesn't affect just local Mass Media, this affects everyone. It will hurt local mainstream harder and earlier, though. Here's why.

Back when I ran an ISP, we talked to the local newspaper about running an ad. The salesperson said we could expect a conversion rate of 4 percent, and that the ad would end up being in front of 100,000 people. Damn that's awesome; 4,000 new customers! We had only 2,000 customers at the time. Except that the print newspaper didn't have any reliable way to track how many people actually saw the ad. The marketing guys claim 4 percent conversion by telling you that you just won't know the new sign-ups are coming from your ad because people won't tell you that's how they found you. Sure, the ad went into 100,000 print newspapers, but there's no way to tell exactly how many people saw it, comprehended it, and acted on it. In our experience the conversion rate was abysmally low; we were told to blame the ad and its placement. A bigger ad with more prominent placement that cost significantly more money would surely do the trick. We declined.

A Mass Media Web site can indeed make effectiveness guarantees. In fact they're required to by online advertisers. The problem with this is that all ad impressions served and clicks on ads are tracked. If an advertiser makes an online ad buy for 100,000 impressions, their ad stays up until all of them are served, not until that day's edition is lining the bottom of the birdcage. If it takes a week, the ad runs for a week.

Marketing experts have been whining and complaining about

poor performance of advertising on the Internet since the beginning. However, I submit to you that perhaps it is really the case that advertising in print and on airwaves has always been just as bad; we just previously had no way to track it. Now we do. The numbers tell us that a successful conversion rate isn't 4 percent, it's 0.2 percent, and that figure doesn't even take into account the number of people who accidentally clicked on the ad trying to find the right-hand slider bar or the big X on the pop-up ad. On top of that, Fark's audience is fairly sophisticated; they won't click ads they don't like. We've had click-through rates on sucky ads that were so low we've been accused of not running the ads at all. Several years ago we signed up with Fastclick.com, purveyor of such masterpiece ads as "Win a Free iPod," "Punch the Monkey to Win," and "You Are the One Millionth Visitor, Click for Your Prize." Let's also not forget the epileptic-fit–inducing shaking ads or "You Have a Virus, Click Here to Remove." Our audience would have none of it, and subsequently our click rate was so low that Fastclick claimed breach of contract and threw us off their ad network. Which was probably just as well; we were getting complaints about their incredibly crappy ads. The quality of a Web site is, therefore, directly impacted by the quality of its advertisements.

The ramifications of all of this: It is highly likely that it may not even be possible to convert newspapers, radio, and TV to the Internet and maintain the same income levels from advertising, because now marketing folks can't lie about how effective it is anymore. And by drop in income, I don't mean a loss of 10 percent; we're talking 90 percent or more. That's a conservative estimate; it could be much worse.

Pre-Internet, Mass Media could charge for ads based on total circulation or viewership whether anyone opened the newspaper to page A5 or actually watched the evening news at 5:42 P.M. Now

Mass Media can charge only if the reader actually reads the specific page in question. Fark's own usage statistics indicate that the average Fark reader clicks on 2 or 3 articles out of 100 main page articles and about 200 sub-page articles. The implication here is that people visiting Mass Media Web sites don't read many of the articles.

Putting it simply: On the Internet, Mass Media can no longer charge money for ads that no one sees. This will drastically reduce available inventory for advertisements. *Drastic* isn't a strong enough word to describe the impact this will have on revenues.

What is the solution for Mass Media here? Barring any other yet-to-be-discovered solutions, I would think any fix to revenue shortfalls would be downsizing and charging more for ads. Maybe some unforeseen innovation will save them all. I'm not holding my breath. Mass Media shouldn't either.

OK, enough of this serious crap. I will swear by this one thing, though: Things are bad but they're no worse than they have been in the past. And in many cases they're a damn sight better.

And now for something completely different to close on...

People frequently ask me what is the weirdest thing I've ever read on Fark. There are a lot of contenders for this honor. The Al Qaida trying and failing to buy nukes from the Russian Mafia is a favorite of mine. I unfortunately can't find it because, back in the day, they were changing the spelling of Al Qaida every other week and you have to spell things correctly to do effective database searches.

There's one, however, that is absolutely burned into my brain for a number of reasons. One, it was one of the first stories we covered back in 1999. Two, it's a This One Time We Were Sooooo Drunk story; those are always classic. Three, it involves a penis. Nothing beats a good penis story. This tops them all.

MAN WHO STAPLED HIS PENIS TO A CROSS AND SET IT ON FIRE IN A BAR BET SAYS HE COULDN'T BE MORE THRILLED TO HAVE RECEIVED AN HONORARY DARWIN AWARD.

In 1999, Trader McKendry's Tavern held a "How Far Will You Go?" promotion. The idea was that people would compete for $500 in cash and a $500 bar tab by basically doing things that would shock and awe the judges. Sounds like a recipe for fun, especially when beer is involved.

Enter Thomas Hendry. We'll cut him some slack here because he was nineteen at the time. I did some pretty stupid stuff when I was nineteen. Not quite this stupid, but not for lack of trying. Actually that's not true; nothing I did could ever come close to this. My friend Phil volunteered for medical experiments, and I thought HE was crazy. So for his entry into the contest, Hendry STAPLED HIS PENIS TO A CRUCIFIX EIGHTEEN TIMES, DOUSED IT WITH LIGHTER FLUID, AND SET IT ON FIRE IN FRONT OF HIS MOM, who was also in attendance at the tavern. Yeah, I used all caps; if there was ever an appropriate time, this is it. She must have been so proud of him. If you really care, you can find pictures of this stunt on the Internet. I don't recommend it. You can live a long and fruitful life without seeing it.

Hendry ended up back in the news seven years later because he had an Honorable Mention Darwin Award bestowed upon him. He was pretty happy about that. He did say that upon further reflection as a twenty-six year-old, he felt it was probably a stupid thing to do. Yes, yes, it was.

In a related story, New Zealand's Broadcasting Standards Authority later ruled that showing footage of a man stapling his penis to a crucifix eighteen times and setting it on fire did not breach good-taste rules. Which begs the question: If that didn't breach good-taste rules, then what on Earth would?

» Randomaccess9999

I thought you didn't get a Darwin unless you died?

» Meshman

From the website: "To qualify for the cult-status United States awards, nominees must have lost their reproductive capacity by killing or sterilising themselves."

» Berylman

I think I know this guy.
  He is going to regret this when the Xanax wears off.

» Berylman

I am guessing it was less of a protest than a statement that simply says "my penis died for your sins." I chart sociological trends as a hobby and I swear to you that within 5 years, there will be snotnose clueless factory-made Christian kids wearing WWMBSCPD (What Would My Burning Stapled Crucifixed Penis Do?) bracelets as they exchange Promise rings and other such nonsensical crap.
  /You don't believe me but you will see.

» Camelclub

Oh Lord, we beseech Thee, take Thine idiot from amongst us.

» Cleveoh

amazingly enough, Ladies, he's still available.

» meekychuppet

He's thrilled because the current rules governing celebrity means he will be getting a TV show and book deal out of this very shortly.

» Petey4335

Well, he just drank a bottle of wine, stapled his penis to a board and set it on fire. If it was me, I'd get it fixed right away. This guy sleeps on it and goes the next day. I'd say he's got balls, but he burnt them.

» Jument

For about a million bucks I'd do something like this to myself. Maybe two million. For $2600 I'd hit myself in the head with a nerf bat (but really hard). This guy is bonzo crazy.

Amusingly the rest of the thread devolved into a religious flamewar. And all was right with the world.

Acknowledgments

Thanks to agent Celeste Fine, who was the person most responsible for this book's current form. Everyone else wanted to do a Best of Fark. I wanted to do a Media Critique. She suggested doing both at the same time. Good idea.

Thanks to Hilary Terrell and the folks at Gotham for all their support. Final products live and die in the editing stage. Thanks for making me look like a good writer. It's just like when I put on a nice suit, suddenly I look legitimate.

Special thanks to Michael Fiegel, who designed the original Fark logo for us. He said his friends didn't believe him, but it's true, he did.

Thanks to Delta Airlines for making every single flight I flew on in 2006 badly late to some degree. Thanks especially for adding eighteen hours to my World Cup 2006 trip; that was the second time in two overseas trips in the same calendar year that I ended up being delayed almost a full day. I did most of the writing for this book on planes; you gave me twice the amount of time I expected to have. I think I shaved a month off the writing time thanks to being late every time I got on a plane. Next book I write, I plan to do the entire thing while flying Delta coach class squeezed between two fat people. Woohoo.

And last but not least, thanks to all the Farkers. Fark is your site; I'm just taking care of it for you. Absolutely none of this, the Web site or the book, would have been possible without you all. FARK ON, BROTHERS AND SISTERS.

Index